Kim Driscoll

una cuoce favolose!

cristina's
tuscan table

Cristina

December. 2007/2008.

First Edition
11 10 09 08 07   5 4 3 2 1

Published by
Gibbs Smith, Publisher
P.O. Box 667
Layton, Utah 84041

Orders: 1.800.835.4993
www.gibbs-smith.com

Designed by Drew Furlong
Printed and bound in China

Library of Congress Cataloging-in-Publication Data

Cook, Cristina Ceccatelli.
Cristina's Tuscan Table / Cristina Ceccatelli Cook;
photographs by Kirsten Shultz.
    p. cm.
Includes index.
ISBN-13: 978-1-4236-0064-0
ISBN-10: 1-4236-0064-9
1. Cookery, Italian—Tuscan style. 2. Food—Italy—Tuscany. I. Title.

TX723.2.T86C66 2007
641.5945'5—dc22
                                    2007015596

cristina's
tuscan table

Cristina Ceccatelli Cook

photography by Kirsten Shultz

Gibbs Smith, Publisher

TO ENRICH AND INSPIRE HUMANKIND

Salt Lake City | Charleston | Santa Fe | Santa Barbara

contents

520 SECOND STREET EAST • 726 4499

acknowledgments

Special thanks to my exceptional customers, whose diversity is surpassed only by their devotion.

To our suppliers and farmers, who bring us the best ingredients ... and always whisper, "What did she say?"

To all my staff, who continue to work in a tiny, tiny kitchen with a crazy "boss" like me;

To my chef, Patrick Jam, for creating extraordinary dishes with simple ingredients;

To Nadina Keller, who wraps our catering orders as though they were leaving Tiffany's;

To my bakers, Alex and Diane, for their beautiful creations, and late nights and early mornings;

To my dishwasher and handyman, Hugo, who has been with me for ten years and still sings every day;

To my front staff managers, Paul Di Ruggiero and Antonio Uriarte, for their sassy repartee;

To my American husband, Steve, whose hair is totally white now, because of me;

To my son, Christopher, for his constant reminder, "Mom, don't have a cow!" (whatever that means);

To my editor, Karen Oswalt, for her passionate patience in making sense of my nonsense;

To Anne Kalik, for her enthusiastic support;

Grazie, grazie mille.

foreword

At the edge of Sun Valley, Idaho, a few miles from where the mountains rise audaciously from the sagebrush to frame the Sawtooth wilderness, there is an intriguing little salmon-colored house. It seems too congenial ever to have been a miner's shack, and far too stationary for the shepherds who moved into the area when silver prices collapsed and sheep became the valley's profit center.

It may be that the house was built in the 1930s, around the time when Averill Harriman pulled into town in his private railroad car—with Bill Paley riding shotgun as his reality check—to sign off on the location for a posh ski resort to enhance passenger traffic on his railroad.

Harriman created Sun Valley, transforming the bucolic little valley into an internationally famous resort, a favorite of corporate moguls and Hollywood grandees, pampered celebrities and wealthy layabouts riding out the Depression.

But the cuisine of central Idaho was, well, primitive. And Harriman's paying guests needed more sophisticated fare to accompany their decidedly un-Idahoan Rob Roys and Bordeaux and martinis.

So hotel chefs were imported . . . several pay levels above the Walter Brennan types serving steak from the back of a chuck wagon out on Trail Creek. But hotel chefs, even with European accents, weren't enough for Sun Valley in the long haul. The well-heeled second-home owners who sailed into town on the golden tide of the 1980s and 90s required far more. Elegant dishes for their "let's lunch" moments. Imaginatively robust fare for after those mornings on the slopes or trout streams or mountain hiking paths. Food with style, served in an atmosphere of mountain clubbiness. Food comparable in quality and élan to what they enjoyed in San Francisco or Paris or Florence.

Fortunately, Cristina showed up to help. A native of Italy, she settled into Sun Valley with her American husband and created, in the little salmon-colored house of vague pedigree, a remarkable restaurant, a center of food and friendship and brio, a place that would have buoyed the spirits of Harriman and Paley.

In the early morning hours the Cristina crowd is focused on newspapers or quiet talk, while being well served by the bakery and kitchen. Some writerly types are regulars, along with an architect or two, and there's always a variety of walk-ins. But lunch is the main event. Local shopkeepers, fly-fishing guides, and athletes mingle with tourists, actors, politicians . . . and perhaps a rancher or two. The little house rattles with rich conversation and laughter.

At night, the restaurant goes dark early as Cristina caters parties for worthy local causes or private celebrations. Her distinctive gift for presentation imbues every event with warmth and flair. Tables are abundant. Decorations are gay. The food is impeccable. And Cristina herself is a presence . . . working at the edge of the event, reassuring the hostess, discreet with the guests, a hawk overseeing the servers and the food.

Quintessentially European, with a touch of mystery, she is lithe and stylish, with great eyes and a sly, beguiling smile. Although thoroughly unassuming, even in kitchen wear she seems startlingly fashionable. No Patagonia or jeans or neon parkas for Cristina. There may be three feet of snow outside, but she seemingly makes it to work in little ballet flats, wearing a cashmere sweater, a colorful skirt and a shawl.

Her style, her persona, were formed by growing up in Tuscany, a place where meals were characterized by energetic conversation and fresh, flavorful food. As they are today in Cristina's little salmon-colored house, at the edge of the Sawtooth Mountains in deepest Idaho.

—Van Gordon Sauter
former president of CBS News
and Fox News

from tuscany to idaho

Long ago, when my grandmother Laurina would exclaim, *"Il Destino! Il Destino! Ha voluto cosi!"* I couldn't imagine the plan that Destiny had written for me.

My story began in the rolling hills of Tuscany, outside Florence. Campaniles, cypress trees, monasteries, and fortresses dotted the hilltops that rose above the lands where wine and olive oil were produced along with tomatoes, tomatoes, and more tomatoes.

Like all Tuscans, we cooked recipes perfected since the time of the Etruscans, prepared from the bounty of our fields, orchards, gardens . . . or from the wild chestnut woods where we found musty truffles, pine nuts, pheasants, and the famous wild boar. Whatever we did not grow ourselves, we bought in the village. The baker, pasta maker, butcher, fruit seller, vegetable vendor, and cheese maker were my extended family. I knew where everything I ate was grown, and who had tended it.

I even knew the source of our drinking water. My handsome Uncle Achille would often take me on the back of his Lambretta to our spring. He would fill two giant ochre jars, and then try to balance them at his feet as we headed back home, bumping along the winding, shady lanes.

In my twenties, I spent my weekends with a Fellini-esque crowd at a villa owned by a character appropriately called *la Nonna Diascola* (the mischievous grandmother). *La Nonna* cut a memorable figure in her big pearls, veiled hat, black Astrakhan coat that barely fit around her ample middle . . . and her signature jewel-encrusted cane. When she settled into her seat in my little Cinquecento Fiat, the car would sink low.

La Nonna reigned over a whirling party of surgeons, artists, students, and wild whatnots. Three generations would stay for a weekend of tennis tournaments, love intrigues, and great cooking.

I watched and learned from her as she bossed the kitchen, sometimes mumbling mysterious incantations into her pots. Perhaps her potions whispered secrets back to her. One night, a beautiful platter of hot risotto was hurled at the unsuspecting head of a cheating husband as he casually walked into the kitchen, expecting his usual good dinner.

On weekdays I taught in Florence, where I met a young American, Jennifer Cook, who was a doctoral student at Harvard's Florence campus. She invited me to visit her family in Boise, Idaho, and I gladly accepted, thrilled to finally visit the "great United States."

Boise in 1981 was a shock for a young woman coming from a Renaissance city of dark, narrow streets, towering palaces, and churches. The open spaces and high desert mountains of Idaho felt uncomfortably strange and overwhelming.

My first visit to an American supermarket was even more shocking. I found Wonder Bread in polka-dot bags, cheese in little squares of plastic. Macaroni in boxes.

Spaghetti already cooked in cans. Grated Parmesan stacked in shiny green cardboard cylinders. I felt as if I'd landed on the moon.

But il Destino had a wonderful American surprise for me ... Steve Cook, Jennifer's brother. I was from Florence. He was from Idaho. It was difficult to imagine two more different backgrounds, but our love linked them, and I settled in Boise, thinking that I would maybe teach Italian.

I had never considered opening a restaurant.

But il Destino stepped in again, and in 1998, with a friend of Steve's, I fell into owning a restaurant. Soon afterward, we relocated to Ketchum, where Steve was working as an architect.

My goal was simple: to re-create an Italian sense of fun and camaraderie, celebrating life with a good meal in good company.

That seemed natural, as in Tuscany our lives were centered around the table. Italians say that spending time at the table brings longevity. Perhaps it's because all the senses come alive with colors, aromas, and tastes, not to mention the joking and laughing. One's troubles are quickly forgotten. The secret is to be a conscious taster rather than a mangione (a big eater) and to leave the table feeling satisfied and grateful for your life. The table is not just about food ... it's about fellowship.

I kept those lessons in mind even as I exchanged Tuscan truffles for Ketchum morels, learned to barbecue cowboy-style and make pigs in a blanket. I once catered a wedding at 8,000 feet in the Boulder Mountains. We got there in jeeps, crossing rocky creeks, as I barely held on to a seven-layer cake. My Uncle Achille would have been proud.

It took awhile to acquire a new palate, but I grew to enjoy peanut butter and jelly sandwiches with my son, Christopher, while he learned to understand and debate the finer points of a carbonara. I have a s'mores pit and, truth be told, I love Twinkies. Not to mention Ho-Hos and jelly beans.

I am still a proud Toscanaccia, or "Tuscan troublemaker," as the other Italians call us. We Tuscans invented the fork, and followed it up with Dante, Michelangelo, Bernini, Cellini, the Medici, and the Renaissance. We think we are such hot stuff that only in Tuscany is the most perfect Italian spoken. We believe in Destiny, pasta, wine, our mothers, friends, love ... and, of course, soccer. We are free-spirited and spontaneous, and we indulge all of the senses. We love, we laugh, we cry, and we pray with great passion.

My grandmother was right. I could never have imagined what my story would be. All in all, I'm glad that il Destino brought me to Ketchum, even though sometimes I still feel a bit like a fish out of water. I love celebrating la dolce vita, Ketchum-style, with a passion for people and life, and food cooked with love.

Come and join us. At my table, there is room for everyone.

—Cristina

antipasti

rosticciana con vino cotto

serves 6 to 8

2 baby rib racks (3 3/4 pounds)

8 sage leaves

3 sprigs fresh rosemary

5 cloves garlic, minced

salt and pepper

3 tablespoons extra virgin olive oil

saba or vino cotto (wine syrup)

Cut the ribs in between the bones. Place in a kitchen bowl with sage, rosemary, garlic, salt and pepper. Drizzle with olive oil and marinate in the refrigerator at least 3 hours or overnight before grilling.

Grill ribs over medium-high heat until crispy on all sides and pink and tender inside, about 25 minutes. Drizzle with Saba or vino cotto and a few drops of olive oil before serving.

Antipasti are really just an ingenious way to use leftovers so everyone can have a taste. From the Italian anti (before) and pasto (food), it literally means "before the meal." Antipasti are like a kiss—a preamble to the main event. The Romans, of course, took antipasti to exuberant extremes, from peacock pâté to pine-nut shortbread. Today's Roman restaurants have beautiful tables, usually set up at the entrance to the dining room, covered with hundreds of antipasto dishes—cured meats, small fishes, figs, grilled meats, and vegetables . . . and on and on.

figs & prosciutto

serves 6 to 8

12 fresh black mission figs or light
    green kadota figs
8 thin slices prosciutto
6 pecans or walnuts, halved
black pepper
vino cotto or balsamic vinegar

Slice figs in half widthwise. Top each half
with a rosette of prosciutto and one
piece of nut. Sprinkle with freshly ground
black pepper and a drop of vino cotto or
balsamic vinegar.

*Figs have played an important part in the
diet and economy of Mediterranean countries for thousands of years. Every stone wall
has its fig tree, and sometimes the ground
around the tree appears to be covered with
fig jam. Before sugar was widely available,
figs were used to preserve cooked fruit. Plato
praised them as "food for athletes," and the
Greeks considered them more precious than
gold. Dried, roasted, or fresh, figs were the
"energy bars" of the Mediterranean people.*

carpaccio di bresaola & roasted beets

serves 6 to 8

3 to 4 medium-sized gold beets
2 tablespoons extra virgin olive oil
$1/2$ pound bresaola, thinly sliced
$1/2$ pound parmigiano, shaved
freshly cracked black pepper
handful of field greens (optional)

Preheat oven to 500° F.

Cover whole beets with cold, salted water and cook over medium-high heat until tender, at least one hour. Drain, and while still hot, remove skin by rubbing beets with a cloth towel. Place beets in a roasting pan, drizzle with olive oil, and roast, turning a few times, until golden brown, about 15 minutes. Remove beets from oven, let cool, then slice thinly and set aside. (This can be done the night before.)

To serve, arrange the beets, bresaola, and shaved parmigiano on a tray. Drizzle with walnut-parsley vinaigrette and add freshly cracked black pepper to taste. Add a few leaves of field greens if you like.

Carpaccio is named after the Renaissance painter Vittore Carpaccio, who was known for his brilliant use of reds and whites. It was created in Harry's Bar in Venice for a contessa whose doctor had placed her on a diet forbidding cooked meat. Carpaccio originally consisted of thinly sliced raw meat.

walnut-parsley vinaigrette

$1/4$ cup toasted walnuts
$3/4$ cup chopped italian parsley
2 teaspoons fresh lemon juice
1 cup extra virgin olive oil
salt and pepper to taste

In a food processor, purée all ingredients.

coccoli

makes 16

3 cups vegetable oil
16 ounces ciabatta dough (p. 207)
kosher salt

In a saucepan, heat the oil to 380° F., measuring temperature using a candy thermometer.

Cut the dough into 16 pieces, handling as little as possible. Gently drop dough, a few pieces at a time, into the oil and cook a few seconds until puffy and golden. Transfer to a paper towel and sprinkle with kosher salt. Repeat until all coccoli are finished.

Serve hot with sliced prosciutto, salami, bresaola, or other cheeses you like. Or try with quince jam, hot candied lemon or orange rinds, truffle honey, or even red pepper jelly.

Coccoli also make a great dessert. Sprinkle hot coccoli with sugar and honey, or serve with ricotta or nutella. Plain is good, too.

Traditionally, bread was made only once or twice a week. Coccoli, *which translates as "chubby little darlings," were made with leftover dough, and the little hot, rough balls became special treats for children.* La mamma fa i coccoli *meant, for us, "Mom, please cuddle me…"*

stuffed piquillo peppers with goat cheese

makes 18

18 roasted (canned or fresh) piquillo peppers

11 ounces goat cheese

$^1/_4$ cup (2 ounces) cream cheese, at room temperature

$^1/_4$ cup milk

2 tablespoons fresh oregano

$^1/_4$ cup toasted pine nuts

salt and pepper to taste

Preheat broiler.

If using canned piquillo peppers, drain and set liquid aside for use in piquillo vinaigrette.

In a food processor using the blade attachment, mix goat cheese, cream cheese, and milk until creamy, about one minute. By hand, stir in oregano, pine nuts, salt and pepper. Place mixture in a pastry bag, and gently distribute the filling into the peppers.

Place stuffed piquillos on a baking sheet, lightly drizzle with 2 tablespoons piquillo vinaigrette, and broil until hot and crispy, about 4 minutes.

Serve peppers drizzled with the remaining vinaigrette and a dollop of olive tapenade.

piquillo vinaigrette

3 tablespoons piquillo pepper liquid

5 tablespoons extra virgin olive oil

3 tablespoons chopped fresh basil

pinch of oregano

salt and freshly cracked black pepper to taste

Whisk all ingredients together.

olive tapenade

$^1/_2$ cup pitted spanish olives

$^3/_4$ cup pitted kalamata olives

1 teaspoon capers

2 teaspoons caper juice

1 clove garlic

In a food processor, blend ingredients only until chunky.

clams & sausages with roasted pepper broth

serves 6 to 8

1 pound red bell peppers, roasted, skins removed, and seeded

10 leaves fresh basil

4 cups chicken or vegetable stock

pinch of salt and pepper

$^1/_4$ cup extra virgin olive oil

2 pounds spicy italian sausage or chorizo, sliced in rounds

$^1/_2$ cup thinly sliced shallots

3 pounds fresh manila clams, cleaned and rinsed

$^1/_4$ cup thinly sliced garlic

1 teaspoon hot red pepper flakes

salt and pepper to taste

sliced, crusty bread

In a food processor, purée first 4 ingredients and set aside.

Heat the olive oil in a large saucepan over medium heat. Cook sausage and shallots together for 3 to 5 minutes. Add clams, garlic, red pepper flakes, salt and pepper, and cook until the garlic is soft, about 2 minutes. Add warm puréed broth, cover, and simmer 3 to 5 minutes until the clams open.

Toast the bread, drizzle with a little olive oil, and serve with clams and sausages.

cod fritters

serves 8

3 cups milk

2 bay leaves

pinch of nutmeg

$^2/_3$ cup white wine

salt and pepper to taste

1 pound fresh cod, washed and
   bones removed

3 cloves garlic, minced and sautéed in
   1 tablespoon olive oil

2 scallions, thinly sliced

$^2/_3$ cup white breadcrumbs

3 tablespoons chopped italian parsley

2 egg yolks

pinch of cayenne

zest of 1 lemon, plus 1 tablespoon
   lemon juice

1 cup light vegetable oil or clarified
   butter for frying

fresh lemon, for garnish

lemon mayonnaise (optional)

tartar sauce (optional)

In a saucepan, bring to boil the milk, bay leaves, nutmeg, wine, salt and pepper, and cod. Reduce heat, and simmer until fish is cooked and flakes away from the skin, about 10 minutes. Leave the fish in the liquid until cool enough to handle, then remove and flake the fish away from the skin. Discard the broth.

Transfer the fish to a bowl and add sautéed garlic, scallions, breadcrumbs, parsley, egg yolks, cayenne, lemon zest, and lemon juice. Adjust taste with salt and pepper and mix well. Refrigerate for 20 minutes; then roll chilled fish mixture into small balls and flatten slightly.

Heat $^1/_4$ cup vegetable oil in a skillet. Fry fritters in batches of 6 to 7, gently turning with a spatula until golden brown. Drain on a paper towel. Add more oil to skillet as needed and heat before frying each batch of fritters. Serve with fresh lemon wedges, tartar sauce, a good, lemony homemade mayonnaise—or just the way they are. If you make the fritters the day before, crisp again on a baking sheet at 500° F. for a few minutes before serving.

These fritters are very good on top of crispy greens with lemon vinaigrette (p. 55), as tiny cocktail sandwiches, or…be creative!

crostini di ricotta e zenzero

makes 15

5 tablespoons fresh ricotta, rolled into 15 balls

1 tablespoon zenzero (finely crushed hot red pepper flakes)

15 bite-sized pieces french or country bread, lightly toasted

2 ripe roma tomatoes, thinly sliced

15 leaves fresh basil

2 tablespoons extra virgin olive oil

pinch of salt

Lightly dip ricotta balls in zenzero and set aside.

Top each piece of bread with a slice of tomato, a basil leaf, and a ricotta ball. Drizzle with olive oil, add salt to taste, and serve.

What exactly are crostini (little crusts) and crostoni (big crusts)? They're just recycled bread. Tuscans consider it a sacrilege to throw out old bread, so we use every last crumb. Yesterday's bread becomes today's creative, crunchy tidbit when toasted and drizzled with excellent olive oil and topped with whatever else you have on hand.

pizzelle e salsa rossa

makes 12

pizzelle

1/4 teaspoon dry yeast

6 tablespoons lukewarm water

1 cup all-purpose flour or pizza flour, divided

4 cups vegetable oil for frying

1/2 cup grated parmigiano

1/2 cup fresh ricotta (optional)

In a small bowl, dissolve yeast in lukewarm water. In a separate mixing bowl, place 1/2 cup flour. Add the yeast mixture to the flour and mix to form a soft, elastic ball of dough. Knead the dough on a floured surface for a few minutes, then cover with a tea towel and let rise in a draft-free place for 2 hours or until doubled in volume.

On a floured surface, using the remaining 1/2 cup flour, roll the dough into a log about 1 inch thick. Cut the log into 1-inch pieces and flatten each piece until very thin.

Heat the oil in a heavy skillet and fry the pizzelle until puffy and golden brown. Drain on a paper towel and transfer to a serving bowl. Top with warm salsa rossa, parmigiano, and dots of fresh ricotta if desired.

salsa rossa

3 tablespoons extra virgin olive oil

1 pound very ripe tomatoes, coarsely chopped

4 cloves garlic, minced

pinch of hot red pepper flakes

10 fresh basil leaves, chopped

salt and pepper to taste

Heat the olive oil in a skillet. Add tomatoes, garlic, and red pepper flakes, and sauté until tomatoes are soft. Stir in fresh basil, and add salt and pepper to taste. Purée or leave chunky and serve on pizzelle.

My regular customers Saul and Shirley Turteltaub wonder . . . "Will they taste the same when we make them? And if they're better, should we tell her?" You decide!

pizza roll-ups

makes 24

2 pizza skins (p. 217)
1/2 cup salsa rossa (p. 35)
1 ball fresh mozzarella, sliced
1/3 cup grated parmigiano
salt and pepper to taste
pinch of hot red pepper flakes
2 tablespoons extra virgin olive oil
1/2 cup chopped fresh basil
handful of fresh arugula (optional)

Preheat oven to 550° F.

Spread pizza skins with salsa rossa up to one inch from rim. Top with mozzarella and sprinkle with parmigiano, salt and pepper, red pepper flakes, and a drizzle of olive oil. Bake on a pizza stone or baking sheet until crispy, about 5 to 6 minutes. Remove from oven and arrange basil and arugula on top.

Cut each crust into 12 wedges and lightly fold to make roll-ups. Serve hot.

Create your own pizza roll-ups with a variety of toppings: try figs, prosciutto, basil, sautéed escarole, and white sauce … roasted eggplant, tomato, caramelized onion, and oregano … gorgonzola, walnuts, grapes, and parsley … artichokes, anchovies, capers, mozzarella, and asiago—pizza!

pizza toscana

serves 8 to 10

3 tablespoons extra virgin olive oil, divided

5 slices day-old country bread, sliced $1/2$ inch thick

$2^1/2$ tablespoons milk

2 cups chopped ripe tomatoes, or canned tomatoes with their juice

2 balls fresh mozzarella, torn in pieces

1 tablespoon capers

5 anchovy fillets (optional)

2 tablespoons fresh oregano

1 teaspoon minced garlic

salt and cracked black pepper to taste

pinch of hot red pepper flakes

Preheat oven to 450° F.

Brush a 12-inch oval casserole dish with one tablespoon olive oil. Arrange the bread to cover bottom of casserole, and drizzle with the milk. Add tomatoes and their juice, mozzarella, capers, anchovy fillets, oregano, and garlic. Finish by drizzling with remaining olive oil and sprinkling with salt and pepper and red pepper flakes, then bake until top is bubbling and crisp, about 45 minutes. Spoon onto plates and serve.

When I am in Italy, my old friend MariaLuisa and I often hold spontaneous cooking classes for her guests at il Leccio, her agriturismo in Strada in Chianti. In her fancy kitchen she has no measuring cups or spoons, and only two knives—but the food always tastes good. We laugh and speak Italian, but her guests have no trouble understanding. They relax, drink good wine, and taste. We know they wonder…how?

MariaLuisa tells me that America is too far away and she is afraid of flying, so our times together are few. Last year before my departure, we cooked ourselves this pizza. We took the pan outside and like two little girls with bad manners we tore it apart— no plates, no forks. Simple food, shared with abandon…life doesn't get any better!

crostini di alici

makes 15

4 tablespoons unsalted butter
15 bite-sized pieces french or country
 bread, lightly toasted
15 white anchovy fillets
15 leaves italian parsley
15 capers (optional)
freshly cracked black pepper

Place a dollop of butter on each crostino. Top each with one white anchovy fillet, a parsley leaf, and a caper. Add black pepper to taste.

white anchovy fillets

8 whole fresh anchovies
juice of 1 lemon
salt and pepper to taste
$1/4$ cup extra virgin olive oil
$1/2$ tablespoon chopped italian parsley

Remove head from fish, then open and remove bones. Wash and pat dry. Arrange the fish fillets on a plate, add lemon juice, and salt and pepper. Cover and refrigerate until white, at least 2 hours. Drain the juice and discard. Drizzle the fillets with olive oil, and sprinkle with parsley.

pane e intingoli mushrooms

makes about 1 cup

5 tablespoons extra virgin olive oil

1/4 pound crimini mushrooms, sliced

1/4 pound chanterelles, sliced

1/4 pound porcini or morels or other
  fresh* mushrooms, sliced

2 teaspoons minced garlic

splash of white wine

2 teaspoons minced italian parsley

1 teaspoon fresh thyme leaves

salt and pepper to taste

pinch of hot red pepper flakes

In a skillet over low heat, sauté the mushrooms in olive oil for about 5 minutes. Add garlic and cook until mushrooms are golden. Add the wine and cook one more minute, then add parsley, thyme, salt and pepper, and red pepper flakes. Cook until mushrooms are soft and juicy. If the mixture gets dry, add 2 tablespoons of the mushroom soaking water or plain water.

Serve with toasted breads, cracker breads, coccoli, flatbreads, old breads, new breads . . .

*If using dried mushrooms, use 6 large morels or 7 to 10 slices porcini. Reconstitute dried mushrooms in warm water. When soft, drain and reserve juice.

pane e intingoli
potato & truffle

makes about 2 cups

1 pound russet potatoes, peeled
2 tablespoons butter
2 teaspoons truffle oil, white or black
salt and pepper to taste
a few shaves of fresh truffle

Place potatoes in a pot of cold, salted water. Bring to a boil, and cook until very soft, reserving $1/4$ cup of the potato water.

In a small bowl, smash the potatoes while hot with a fork. Mix in the butter, truffle oil, and salt and pepper. Add shaved fresh truffle and a little potato water, if the mixture needs moisture.

Serve with toasted breads.

scampi al dragoncello

serves 8

24 large shrimp, cleaned and deveined,
  tails left on

$^1/_4$ cup extra virgin olive oil, plus
  2 tablespoons for frying

juice and zest of 2 oranges

juice and zest of $^1/_2$ lemon

2 tablespoons fresh tarragon leaves

1 teaspoon crushed garlic

$^1/_4$ teaspoon hot red pepper flakes

1 tablespoon chopped italian parsley

a few sprigs fresh tarragon, for garnish

a few orange slices, for garnish

Combine shrimp, $^1/_4$ cup olive oil, juice
and zest of oranges and lemon, tarragon,
garlic, red pepper flakes, and parsley in a
bowl. Refrigerate at least 30 minutes.

In a skillet, heat 2 tablespoons olive oil
and cook the shrimp on high heat for 3
to 5 minutes, adding a splash of marinade
as you cook to keep them moist.

Serve hot, garnished with fresh tarragon
sprigs and orange slices.

This shrimp also makes a great topping
for greens, tomato salad, or pasta. If using
for pasta, add a splash of white wine to
the shrimp while cooking. Stir the shrimp
into the cooked pasta, along with 2 more
pinches of parsley and tarragon.

cauliflower &
fennel tasty plate

makes 5 cups

3/4 cup diced pancetta (6 to 7 ounces)

1 small head cauliflower

1 bulb fresh fennel

2 cloves garlic, minced

1/2 cup goat cheese

1/4 cup gorgonzola cheese

3/4 cup grated parmigiano, plus
   2 tablespoons for topping

1/2 cup sour cream

3 tablespoons chopped italian parsley

salt and pepper to taste

2 tablespoons breadcrumbs,
   for topping

Preheat oven to 400° F.

In a large skillet, cook pancetta over medium heat until lightly browned. Set aside.

Wash cauliflower and discard the stem. Break into chunks and cook in boiling salted water until soft. Drain.

Wash the fennel, then cut off and discard upper stalks. Remove any wilted outer layers from the bulb, and cut a thin slice from the fennel base and discard. Cut the fennel in half lengthwise, then cut (lengthwise again) into very thin slices.

Add the cauliflower and fennel to the pancetta pan and cook on medium heat until vegetables are lightly browned, about 5 or 6 minutes. Stir in garlic and cook a few more minutes.

Remove from heat and transfer into a bowl. Add the cheeses, sour cream, parsley, salt and pepper, and mix just enough to combine. Transfer the mixture to an ovenproof 6 x 6-inch casserole, top with breadcrumbs and 2 tablespoons parmigiano, and bake, uncovered, for about 15 minutes or until top is lightly browned.

Serve with crudités of vegetables and, of course, breads.

salads

orzo, corn & avocado salad

serves 8

1 pound orzo

3 tablespoons extra virgin olive oil, divided

1 cup fresh corn

4 avocados

$1/3$ cup lime juice, divided

7 scallions, sliced in thin rounds

2 tablespoons chopped italian parsley

zest of 2 limes

salt and pepper to taste

Cook pasta until al dente. Drain and set aside.

In a skillet, heat one tablespoon olive oil over high heat, add the fresh corn, and sauté until light brown. Set aside to cool.

Remove skin from avocados, cube pulp, and drizzle with one tablespoon lime juice to prevent discoloration.

In a mixing bowl, gently combine cooked orzo, corn, avocado, scallions, parsley, lime zest, remaining lime juice, remaining 2 tablespoons olive oil, and salt and pepper. Taste, and add more lime juice if you like.

Serve on radicchio di treviso or on beautiful, ripe tomatoes. This crispy, light salad also makes an excellent side dish for all your barbecued meats or chicken.

Whatever became of a salad of simple greens? Fresh, beautiful, and crispy. To make an easy, flavorful dressing, do as my father Emilio does: On a soup spoon, dissolve a pinch of salt in a bit of red wine vinegar and whisk it with a fork. Sprinkle it over your greens and follow with a drizzle of olive oil and freshly cracked pepper. Toss and enjoy. Now that's a salad!

In Florence we say, "L'olio d'oliva, l'aceto di vino, il sale e pepe, fanno buono anche lo stivale." ("Olive oil, vinegar, salt, and pepper will make even a boot taste good.")

celery, hazelnut & pecorino salad

serves 6

3 celery hearts and tender pale
   green leaves

2 cups toasted hazelnuts, coarsely
   crushed

2 pounds brinata* cut in $1/2$-inch cubes

30 whole leaves italian parsley,
   for garnish

freshly cracked black pepper

Cut celery hearts into $1/2$-inch crescents
and coarsely chop the pale green leaves.

In a salad bowl, mix celery, toasted
hazelnuts, and brinata. Lightly toss with
lemon vinaigrette, garnish with parsley
leaves, and serve with freshly cracked
black pepper.

*Brinata is a young Tuscan pecorino, mild
and soft. Its natural, edible rind is encrusted
with a delicate white mold, like felt.
Brinata is very good served with quince,
truffle honey, fig mustard, almond or chestnut honey…and, of course, with pears or
fava beans.*

toasted hazelnuts

Preheat oven to 500° F.

On a baking sheet, bake nuts 4 to 5 minutes, then rub with a clean towel until
skin is almost all gone. On a flat surface,
crush nuts into large pieces. We do it by
rocking the bottom of a heavy skillet
over the nuts.

lemon vinaigrette

makes 1 cup

$1/2$ cup extra virgin olive oil

$1/2$ cup freshly squeezed lemon juice

$1/2$ cup finely chopped italian parsley

1 tablespoon brown sugar

salt and pepper to taste

Whisk together all ingredients.

Lemon vinaigrette is good warm or cold,
on fish, salads, chicken, or fruit.

grilled zucchini & "drunken" pecorino

serves 6 to 8

4 medium zucchini

4 yellow squash

$^3/_4$ pound pecorino brillo*, thinly
    sliced, rind removed

1 tablespoon minced garlic

$^1/_3$ cup minced italian parsley

4 tablespoons extra virgin olive oil

juice and zest of 1 lemon

salt and pepper to taste

Cut zucchini and squash lengthwise into
$^1/_8$-inch slices. Grill until grill marks are
visible.

In a serving bowl, toss zucchini, squash,
pecorino, garlic, parsley, olive oil, and
lemon juice and zest. Taste for salt and
pepper.

*Pecorino is made from sheep's milk.
Tuscany has thousands of great pecorinos, the most famous made in Pienza and
Mugello. Fresh, aged, drunken...aged in
caves, barrels, burlap...I could write and
write about these pecorinos! The brillo, or
"drunken," is aged four months, and then
the wheels are washed, dried, and placed
in terra-cotta containers with wine for one
more month. At this point, the cheese is
monitored daily until it reaches the perfect absorption of the wine, which gives it
a delicate fragrance.

smashed tomato caesar

serves 6

6 large, ripe tomatoes, cut in chunks

6 romaine hearts, torn

3 cups croutons

1$^1/_2$ cups grated parmigiano

salt and freshly cracked black pepper to taste

anchovy fillets, for garnish (optional)

6 lemon wedges, for garnish

Prepare caesar dressing and refrigerate until ready to use.

In a salad bowl, smash tomato chunks with a fork, reserving all juices.

To serve, pour one cup caesar dressing into bowl with tomatoes, add torn romaine, croutons, one cup parmigiano, and toss. Adjust for salt and pepper. Garnish with anchovy fillets, lemon wedges, and remaining parmigiano.

caesar dressing

makes about 2 cups

1 egg, plus 2 yolks

2 cloves garlic, chopped

1$^1/_2$ teaspoons dijon mustard

2 anchovy fillets

juice of 1$^1/_2$ lemons

1 tablespoon red wine vinegar

1$^1/_2$ tablespoons worcestershire sauce

dash of tabasco

white pepper to taste

1$^1/_2$ cups extra virgin olive oil

In a food processor with a blade attachment, blend egg and yolks with garlic until thickened. Add mustard and anchovies and mix until puréed. Mix in lemon juice, vinegar, worcestershire, tabasco, and dash of white pepper. Keeping the motor running, slowly pour in olive oil. Consistency should be like heavy cream, smooth and pourable.

scallops, zucchini & pears

serves 6

2 pounds u-10 sea scallops
(about 18 scallops)

1 tablespoon grated fresh ginger

1 tablespoon minced chives, plus
2 tablespoons for garnish

1 tablespoon minced garlic

2 tablespoons sesame oil

salt and pepper to taste

3 anjou pears, quartered and cored

6 zucchini, sliced lengthwise in
$^1/_4$-inch strips

4 yellow crookneck squash, sliced
lengthwise in $^1/_4$-inch strips

2 leeks, tops removed, sliced
lengthwise in $^1/_4$-inch strips

$^1/_4$ cup extra virgin olive oil

In a bowl, combine scallops, ginger, one tablespoon chives, garlic, sesame oil, salt and pepper, and refrigerate one hour.

While scallops are marinating, heat a flat-top grill to very hot. Coat pears, zucchini, squash, and leeks with olive oil and sprinkle with salt and pepper. Grill on both sides until grill marks are visible and vegetables are soft. Set aside and keep warm.

In a skillet over medium-high heat, sear scallops with their marinade, 2 minutes per side.

To serve, arrange grilled vegetables on plates and top with 3 scallops each. Drizzle with ginger-sherry sauce and garnish with minced chives.

ginger-sherry sauce

1 tablespoon butter

2 tablespoons grated fresh ginger

1 tablespoon minced garlic

salt and white pepper to taste

$^1/_2$ cup dry sherry

juice of $^1/_2$ lemon

2 cups heavy cream

In a saucepan over low heat, melt butter. Stir in ginger, garlic, salt and white pepper, and cook one minute. Add dry sherry and flambé. Add lemon juice, then slowly stir in cream, cooking one more minute.

I have discovered many ingredients in this country that do not appear in traditional Tuscan cooking—or in Italian cooking, for that matter. I would say that this dish is Tuscan in sensibility, spirit, and exuberance. Our customers love it.

fall salad

serves 6

1 head butter lettuce, outer leaves removed	In a bowl, gently tear butter lettuce and mix with arugula.

1 head butter lettuce, outer leaves
   removed

¹/₄ pound fresh arugula

18 fresh figs, halved

1 burrata* (about 1 pound) or fresh
   mozzarella, torn or sliced

¹/₂ cup pecan or walnut halves

lemon vinaigrette (p. 55)

freshly cracked black pepper

few drops vino cotto (optional)

In a bowl, gently tear butter lettuce and mix with arugula.

On a serving platter, arrange greens, figs, burrata, and nuts. Drizzle with lemon vinaigrette, add freshly cracked black pepper, and—if you want to be extravagant—a few drops of vino cotto.

Add a slice of good bread and forget traditions…the grandmothers…art… Tuscans…it's just a simple lunch or dinner!

Burrata is a cheese formed by wrapping a creamy Stracciatella center with a fleshy outer layer of fresh mozzarella, resulting in a large ball weighing one pound. This robust cheese is creamy and dense and is best enjoyed naturally or dressed with a little salt, black pepper, and olive oil. Arugula is a good match for Burrata.

grilled chicken
cobb salad

serves 6

6 half chicken breasts
  (about 1 pound), lightly pounded

1/4 cup extra virgin olive oil

2 sprigs fresh rosemary

2 tablespoons minced garlic

salt and pepper to taste

3 avocados

juice of 2 limes

12 slices bacon

1 head butter lettuce, outer leaves
  removed

1 pound field greens

1 1/2 cups sliced scallions

6 roma tomatoes, cubed

16 ounces blue cheese, crumbled

6 hard-boiled eggs, quartered

In a bowl, mix together chicken, olive oil, rosemary, garlic, salt and pepper, and let marinate while you prepare the remainder of the salad.

Peel avocados, cut in slices, sprinkle with lime juice, and set aside.

In a skillet over medium heat, crisp bacon until fat is rendered. Remove from pan, drain on a paper towel, and cut in small pieces.

In a salad bowl, gently tear butter lettuce (avoid bruising), add field greens, scallions, tomatoes, blue cheese, avocados, bacon, and eggs.

In a hot skillet, cook chicken breasts in their marinade until golden on both sides and juicy inside. Remove from pan and slice in long strips.

To serve, lightly toss salad greens with cobb vinaigrette (p. 67), top with hot chicken, adjust for pepper, and serve with flatbread.

cobb vinaigrette

makes 2 cups

$1/2$ cup water

$1/2$ cup red wine vinegar

$1/2$ teaspoon sugar

juice of $1/2$ lemon

1 teaspoon salt

$1/2$ teaspoon freshly cracked
   black pepper

$1 1/2$ teaspoons worcestershire sauce

$1/2$ teaspoon dijon mustard

1 clove garlic, minced

$3/4$ cup extra virgin olive oil

Whisk together until blended.

Mrs. Puchner—or Ann, as her friends call her—has been supporting us for many years. She is a fabulous cook, and grows beautiful berries and herbs. We make great tarts with her gooseberries. She gave us the recipe for Cobb Vinaigrette and we use it all the time. You can add a little horseradish, or orange juice, or hot pepper sauce—it's always fantastic!

seared ahi with asian slaw

serves 6

1 cup sesame seeds

$^1/_4$ cup wasabi powder

$1^1/_2$ tablespoons sugar

pinch of salt and pepper

$1^1/_2$ pounds sushi-grade ahi in a block

$1^1/_2$ tablespoons water

$^1/_4$ cup clarified butter

In a mixing bowl, combine sesame seeds, wasabi powder, sugar, salt and pepper. Mix in water.

Coat top and bottom of ahi block in sesame seed mixture, pressing down to make sure it sticks. Cut ahi in 6 pieces widthwise, and refrigerate while you prepare the asian slaw, slaw vinaigrette, and wasabi drizzle (p. 71).

In a skillet over high heat, heat clarified butter. Add coated ahi and cook one minute on each side. Remove from pan and slice each piece widthwise into one-inch chunks.

To serve, arrange slaw, lightly coated with its vinaigrette, on a plate. Top with hot ahi chunks and drizzle with wasabi. Garnish with pickled cucumber (p. 71), and pickled ginger.

If you have your slaw, vinaigrette, and wasabi drizzle ready, this salad is a piece of cake. If you don't... order a good take-out and make this salad the next day!

asian slaw

1/2 cup thinly sliced red cabbage

2 cups thinly sliced napa cabbage

1 medium carrot, shaved lengthwise

1 zucchini, cut in thin rounds

1 yellow crookneck squash, cut in thin rounds

1 1/2 cups snap peas, string removed, blanched, and halved on diagonal

1/2 cup cilantro leaves

In a bowl, toss all ingredients together.

slaw vinaigrette

1/4 cup wasabi paste

2/3 cup honey

1 cup rice vinegar

2 tablespoons picked ginger juice

juice of 1/2 lemon

1/3 cup vegetable oil

1 tablespoon black sesame seeds

Whisk ingredients together.

wasabi drizzle

1/4 cup wasabi paste

1 1/2 cups pickled ginger, juice reserved

3 cups mayonnaise

3/4 cup pickled ginger juice

1/3 cup sesame oil

In a food processor with a blade attachment, blend ingredients until creamy. If stored in the refrigerator, wasabi drizzle will last at least a month. It's very good for vegetable dip, chicken, fish, or...

pickled cucumber

1 english cucumber, cut in 1/8-inch rounds

1/2 cup rice vinegar

1/4 cup sugar

1/2 teaspoon hot red pepper flakes

Soak cucumber in rice vinegar, sugar, and red pepper flakes. Store in the juice and use within 2 days.

cannellini beans, calamari & spinach salad

serves 6

6 calamari steaks
  (about 1 1/2 pounds), pounded

1/4 cup extra virgin olive oil

2 tablespoons chopped italian parsley

1 tablespoon chopped garlic

1 tablespoon chopped chives

1 teaspoon hot red pepper flakes

2 lemons, cut in wedges

pinch of salt and pepper

1 pound fresh baby spinach

Prepare the cannellini beans, fire oil, and fire vinaigrette (p. 75), in advance.

Place calamari steaks, olive oil, parsley, garlic, chives, and red pepper flakes in a bowl and marinate, refrigerated, for 30 minutes.

Heat a cast-iron flat-top grill to very hot. Grill steaks 2 minutes, squeeze lemon wedges over the top, then flip. Salt and pepper the cooked side. Cook one more minute and squeeze with lemon. Remove from grill and salt and pepper the other side. Cut into 4 to 5 slices.

On a serving dish, arrange spinach and hot cannellini beans, and top with calamari. Drizzle with fire vinaigrette. Serve with a chunk of ciabatta.

cannellini beans

2 cups dried cannellini beans

2 tablespoons chopped garlic

4 sage leaves

2 bay leaves

$^1/_2$ cup extra virgin olive oil

1 $^1/_2$ cups chopped roma tomatoes

salt and pepper to taste

$^1/_4$ cup chopped italian parsley

Soak beans overnight in 6 cups cold, salted water.

Drain, rinse, and place in a pot with 8 cups cold, salted water. Add garlic, sage leaves, bay leaves, olive oil, tomatoes, salt and pepper, and bring to boil. Cover and cook on low simmer for 3 to 4 hours or until soft. Add parsley.

fire oil

1 cup extra virgin olive oil

1 tablespoon hot red pepper flakes

2 cloves garlic

In a saucepan, heat olive oil over low heat, add red pepper flakes and garlic, and let infuse 45 minutes. Cool before using in fire vinaigrette.

fire vinaigrette

1 teaspoon dijon mustard

$^1/_4$ cup water

1 cup fire oil

$^1/_2$ cup vegetable oil

juice of 1 lemon

$^1/_2$ tablespoon minced garlic

$^1/_2$ teaspoon hot red pepper flakes

1 tablespoon fresh oregano leaves

pinch of salt

Whisk ingredients together.

panzanella

serves 6

1 1/2 cups cold water

1/2 loaf day-old crusty country bread, cut in thick slices

6 large vine-ripened tomatoes, cut in wedges, juice reserved

1 medium english cucumber, sliced

1 medium red onion, sliced in thin crescents

1/2 cup fresh basil, chopped

18 caperberries or capers

salt and pepper to taste

fresh arugula (optional)

anchovy fillets (optional)

In a shallow bowl, pour water over bread and let rest for about 15 minutes, or until water is absorbed. Using your hands, squeeze the water out of the bread and then transfer to a salad bowl. Bread should be soft and chunky.

Add tomatoes and their juice, cucumber, onion, basil, caperberries, and salt and pepper. Add arugula and anchovy fillets, if using, and toss with basil vinaigrette.

basil vinaigrette

1 cup fresh basil, finely chopped

1/2 cup extra virgin olive oil

splash of lemon juice

splash of red wine vinegar or sherry vinegar

1 teaspoon dijon mustard

pinch of salt and pepper

Whisk all ingredients together.

The simpler, the better. The real panzanella has no anchovies, roasted peppers, or any other embellishments...and the traditional dressing is olive oil, red vinegar, salt and pepper.

soups

cipollata

serves 10

3/4 cup extra virgin olive oil, divided

6 yellow onions, cut in 1/4-inch
  crescents

2 russet potatoes, skins on,
  cut in 1-inch cubes

3 bay leaves

pinch of nutmeg

salt and pepper to taste

1 gallon beef or vegetable stock,
  warmed

10 slices day-old country bread,
  toasted and broken in half

3/4 cup grated parmigiano

In a soup pot, heat 1/2 cup olive oil over medium heat. Add the onions and cook until translucent, about 10 to 15 minutes. Increase heat to medium-high, add remaining 1/4 cup olive oil, and continue stirring until onions are caramelized, about 30 minutes. Add potatoes, bay leaves, nutmeg, salt and pepper. Continue to stir and cook 5 more minutes. Add warm broth and simmer, covered, until potatoes are soft, about one hour.

To serve, in ovenproof soup bowls layer the broth, bread, and parmigiano. Repeat the layers, then broil for a few minutes until tops are golden.

This rustic soup from Tuscany traveled to France with Caterina dei Medici and became, after transformation by the French, their famous soupe d'oignons. Caterina was only 14 years old when she was married to Prince Enrico d'Orleans. She arrived in France accompanied by her cooks, nannies, alchemist, and servants— and all the traditions of her Tuscan kitchens. Her cooks kept cooking and the politicians kept eating and soon, as the story goes, the clever Caterina became a powerful political figure. Because of her Italian heritage, she knew that nothing is more effective than discussing important political matters with your feet under a well-furnished table.

tuscan fish stew

serves 10

1 $^{1}/_{4}$ pounds halibut or white fish,
   cut in 1-inch cubes

1 pound medium shrimp, shelled,
   deveined, and cut in half lengthwise

1 pound large scallops, halved

1 tablespoon fresh tarragon leaves

1 tablespoon fresh dill

1 tablespoon fresh thyme leaves

1 teaspoon celery salt

$^{1}/_{4}$ teaspoon hot red pepper flakes

1 tablespoon minced garlic

$^{1}/_{4}$ cup extra virgin olive oil

1 cup white wine

6 cups seafood broth (p. 85)

$^{3}/_{4}$ cup grated parmigiano (optional)

whole italian parsley leaves,
   for garnish

In a large bowl, combine the seafood with the 6 herbs and the olive oil. Marinate in the refrigerator while you prepare the seafood broth.

In a large skillet over high heat, sauté the seafood and its marinade in batches until light gold in color but not cooked through, about 3 to 5 minutes. Add a little white wine after each batch to deglaze the pan; repeat until all the seafood is cooked.

Add the sautéed seafood and juices to the simmering broth, cook for 5 minutes, and serve garnished with parmigiano and whole parsley leaves.

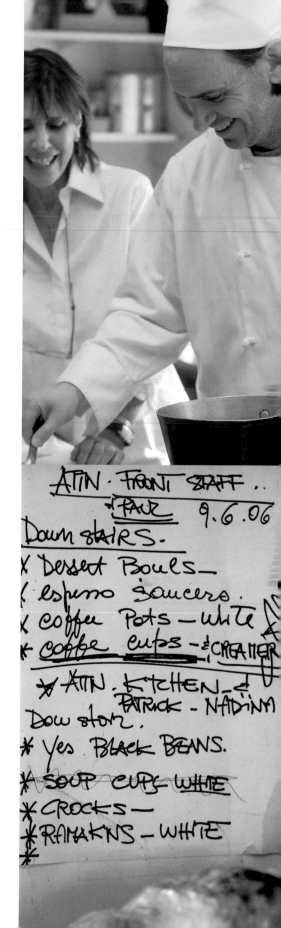

seafood broth

$^1/_4$ cup extra virgin olive oil

1 cup thinly sliced leeks,
  white part only

1 cup thinly sliced red onion

1 cup thinly sliced celery

2 carrots, thinly sliced in $^1/_2$ rounds
  (1 cup)

$^1/_2$ fennel bulb, sliced in thin crescents

6 cups diced tomatoes, fresh or canned,
  with their juice

6 cups fish stock

3 bay leaves

salt and pepper to taste

In a soup pot, heat olive oil. Add leeks, red onion, celery, carrots, and fennel. Stirring once or twice, sauté for 15 minutes or until vegetables are soft and golden. Add tomatoes with their juice, fish stock, bay leaves, and salt and pepper. Simmer for 30 minutes.

fish stock

makes 6 cups

$^1/_4$ pound halibut or
  white fish with bones

shells from 1 pound shrimp

greens from 2 leeks

2 stalks celery, coarsely chopped

stalks and outer leaves of 1 fennel bulb

1 lemon, quartered

2 bay leaves

6 peppercorns

6 cloves garlic

3 roma tomatoes or 1 large tomato,
  cut in half

1 teaspoon fennel seed

1 teaspoon celery seed

10 cups water

1 tablespoon lobster concentrate

salt and pepper to taste

In a large stockpot, bring all ingredients to a boil and simmer for 30 to 45 minutes. Strain. Broth can be frozen.

tortellini in brodo

serves 10

$^{1}/_{4}$ cup extra virgin olive oil

5 cups diced yellow onions

3 cups diced carrots

3 cups diced celery

$^{1}/_{2}$ cup chopped italian parsley

1 tablespoon fresh thyme leaves

4 bay leaves

salt and pepper to taste

1 gallon chicken stock, warmed

2 pounds fresh tortellini (any flavor)

1 cup grated parmigiano

In a soup pot, heat olive oil, then add onions, carrots, and celery. Sauté about 10 minutes, stirring once or twice, until onions are translucent. Add parsley, thyme, bay leaves, salt and pepper, and cook for 3 minutes. Add the chicken stock, bring to a boil, and simmer at least 20 minutes. Add the tortellini, reduce heat, and cook until pasta floats.

Serve with grated parmigiano.

roasted pepper
& tomato soup

serves 10

20 red bell peppers or 2 (1-pound) cans roasted red bell peppers

1/2 cup extra virgin olive oil, divided

salt and pepper to taste

30 roma tomatoes, cut in half lengthwise

1 yellow onion, coarsely chopped

1/2 tablespoon minced garlic

2 tablespoons chopped fresh basil

2 tablespoons fresh thyme leaves

2 cups vegetable stock (p. 91)

crème fraîche, for garnish

a few sprigs fresh thyme, for garnish

a few basil leaves, for garnish

Preheat oven to 550° F.

If using fresh peppers: layer peppers on a baking sheet, drizzle with 2 tablespoons olive oil, and sprinkle with salt and pepper. Roast until skin is slightly charred and flaking off the pulp, about 20 minutes, turning a few times.

Transfer peppers and their juices into a kitchen bowl. Cover with clear plastic and let steam for a few minutes. Remove skins and seeds. Set peppers aside in a bowl with their juices. Roast tomatoes with skins on until charred. Remove from oven and set aside.

In a saucepan, heat the remaining olive oil. Add onion and sauté until soft and translucent. Add garlic, basil, and thyme, and cook 2 more minutes. Stir in the roasted peppers and tomatoes with all their juices, and simmer 2 more minutes. Salt and pepper to taste. Add vegetable stock and simmer 5 more minutes.

In a food processor, purée mixture in batches, then return to pot and reheat before serving. Garnish with a sprig of thyme, a leaf of basil, and a dollop of crème fraîche.

vegetable stock

makes about a 1 1/2 gallons

2 potatoes, unpeeled

1 onion

2 carrots, unpeeled

2 stalks celery

handful of any greens—
   kale, escarole, spinach

2 bay leaves

4 basil leaves

4 sprigs italian parsley

4 sprigs thyme

4 sprigs marjoram

fennel trimmings (optional)

2 cloves garlic

4 peppercorns

salt and pepper to taste

2 gallons cold water

Cut vegetables into large chunks and place in a large soup pot with the herbs, salt and pepper, and water. Bring to a boil and simmer for 1 hour. Strain and refrigerate or freeze stock for use in soups and sauces.

Italians are the masters of leftovers, so we do not have specific vegetable- or meat-stock recipes. Everything that needs to be used goes in the pot…and that is why your broth will taste different every time.

Quintilia, my grandmother's cook, used to remind us that il popolo (the common people) and i sapienti (city hall)—everyone, in other words—know that to make a good stock we need to place the vegetables in a pot of cold water and let simmer very slowly. But for a good boiled meat, we have to add the meat to already-simmering water.

butternut squash soup with pears, apples & leeks

serves 10

2 tablespoons extra virgin olive oil

2 tablespoons butter

$^1/_2$ cup thinly sliced leeks

$^3/_4$ cup cubed apples
   (save core for stock)

$^3/_4$ cup cubed pears
   (save core for stock)

1 tablespoon chopped fresh sage
   leaves (reserve stalks for stock)

$^1/_2$ tablespoon fresh thyme leaves
   (reserve stalks for stock)

$^1/_4$ cup marsala or madeira wine

12 cups apple-pear stock (p. 95)

5 cups roasted butternut squash (p. 95)

salt and pepper to taste

10 pear slices, sautéed in butter,
   for garnish

sage leaves, for garnish

In a soup pot, heat olive oil and butter. Add leeks, apples, and pears. Sauté over medium heat until leeks are translucent, about 3 to 5 minutes. Stir in sage and thyme, and cook for 2 more minutes. Add wine, simmer a few minutes, then add apple-pear stock and roasted butternut squash. Simmer for one hour. Add salt and pepper to taste, then serve with sautéed pears and sage leaves. If you prefer a thicker soup, cook 20 minutes longer.

Leftover soup, with a little added cream and parmigiano, makes a great sauce for cheese ravioli.

In Florence, we find squashes from September to January. We dry the seeds in the oven, sprinkle with a little salt...and that's our popcorn. We chew on the semi di zucca *at the movies. They are good...but oh, how these seeds make me thirsty!*

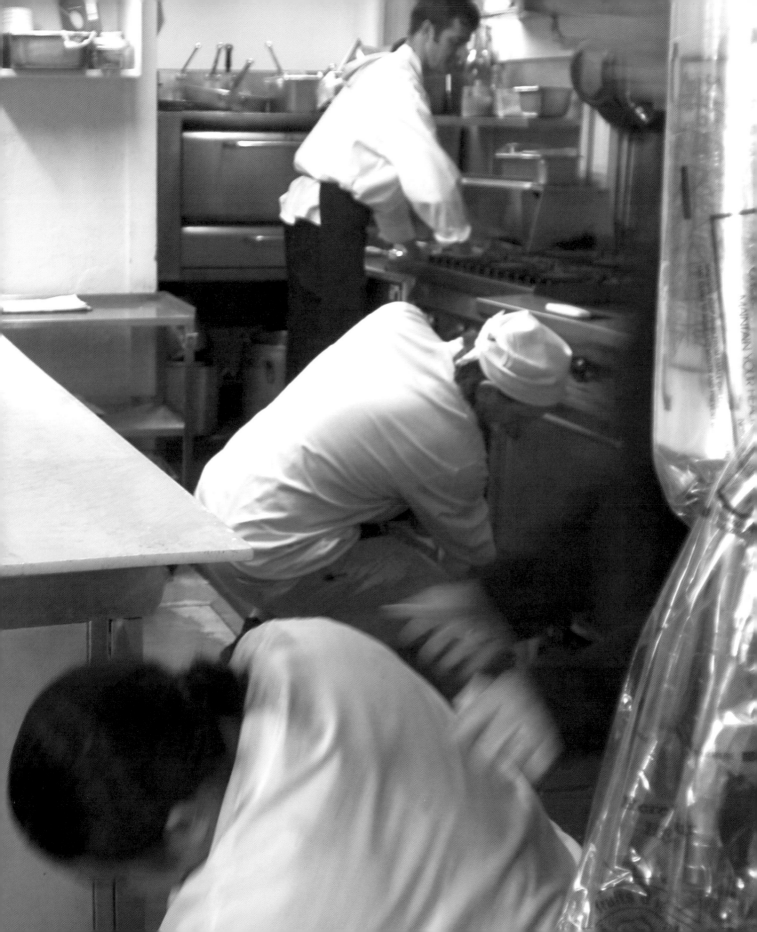

roasted butternut squash

makes 5 or 6 cups

3 large butternut squash
$^1/_2$ tablespoon fresh thyme leaves
1 tablespoon chopped sage leaves
$^1/_2$ tablespoon chopped garlic
salt and pepper to taste
$^1/_4$ cup extra virgin olive oil
pinch of cinnamon (optional)

Preheat oven to 450° F.

Cut squash in half lengthwise, seed, and place on a baking sheet, skin side down. Sprinkle with thyme, sage, garlic, salt and pepper, and cinnamon. Drizzle with $^1/_4$ cup olive oil.

Roast for 1 $^1/_2$ hours or until soft. Let cool, then scoop out squash from skin.

apple-pear stock

2 gallons water
1 apple core
1 pear core
4 small leeks, green part only
4 stalks celery
2 cloves garlic
4 bay leaves
2 sprigs each thyme and sage
$^1/_2$ teaspoon celery seed
$^1/_2$ teaspoon fennel seed
$^1/_2$ teaspoon nutmeg
2 tablespoons maple syrup

In a stockpot, bring ingredients to a rolling boil, then simmer for 30 minutes. Strain and reserve stock.

chilled avocado soup

serves 6

8 avocados, peeled and pitted

8 scallions, chopped

4 tablespoons lemon juice

4 cups vegetable stock (p. 91), chicken stock, or water

1 1/2 teaspoons chile powder

1 teaspoon salt

1/2 teaspoon cumin

1/2 teaspoon coriander

Purée avocados and scallions. Mix in remaining ingredients and chill well. Serve topped with tomato-cucumber salsa.

tomato-cucumber salsa

5 roma tomatoes, diced

1 cucumber, diced

1 jalapeño, seeded and minced

1 1/2 teaspoons chopped cilantro

1 1/2 teaspoons lemon juice

2 cloves garlic, minced

pinch of salt

Combine all ingredients and adjust for salt.

spicy cream of pepper soup

serves 10

$^1/_2$ cup butter

3 cups chopped green bell peppers

1 cup chopped carrots

5 cups chopped yellow onions

2 jalapeños, seeded and diced

1$^1/_2$ cups all-purpose flour

1 tablespoon coriander seed

pinch of salt and pepper

13 cups chicken stock or vegetable stock (p. 91)

1 quart heavy cream

a few slices mimolette* or shaved cheddar, for garnish

a few scallions, for garnish

In a saucepan, heat the butter, peppers, carrots, onions, and jalapeños, and sauté until onions are translucent, about 5 to 7 minutes. Stir in flour, coriander, salt and pepper, and cook 2 minutes. Add stock and cream, bring to a boil, and simmer 30 to 40 minutes. Let cool; then purée. Adjust for salt and pepper. Serve hot, garnished with mimolette and a few sliced scallions.

Make this soup as spicy as you like it by adjusting jalapeños.

*aged Normandy cheddar

If you like peppers, you will like this soup. Should you decide to substitute half-and-half or milk for the heavy cream, the soup will be less creamy and more brothy. You decide! Experiment, taste, and most important—don't forget to laugh!

matteo's carrot & ginger soup

serves 6

8 cups peeled, coarsely chopped carrots

10 cups vegetable stock (p. 91)

$^1/_2$ cup grated fresh ginger

1 tablespoon butter

$^1/_2$ small yellow onion, diced

1 $^1/_2$ tablespoons soy sauce

$^1/_2$ tablespoon dried ginger

$^1/_2$ tablespoon pickled ginger juice

$^1/_3$ cup smooth peanut butter

salt and white pepper to taste

peanuts and pickled ginger, for garnish

In a large pot, bring carrots, vegetable stock, and fresh ginger to a boil. Let simmer until carrots are soft, about 40 minutes. Remove from heat and let cool.

While the carrots are cooking, sauté the diced onion in the butter until soft and translucent. Add sautéed onion to the cooked carrots. In a food processor, purée the carrot mixture a little at a time. Pour the carrots back into the stockpot and add the soy sauce, dried ginger, ginger juice, peanut butter, and salt and pepper. Bring to a simmer over low heat, stirring with a wooden spoon until the peanut butter is completely blended in and there are no lumps.

Serve garnished with a few peanuts and pickled ginger.

zuppa di farro

serves 10

1 cup farro

2 tablespoons extra virgin olive oil

1 cup thinly sliced celery

3/4 cup thinly sliced fresh fennel, stalks and outer leaves removed

1 cup diced red onions

salt and pepper to taste

1 cup carrot matchsticks

4 cups chopped fresh tomatoes, with their juices

2 bay leaves

1 gallon vegetable stock (p. 91)

1/2 tablespoon fresh tarragon leaves

2 handfuls lacinato kale, escarole, or spinach, coarsely chopped

1/4 cup chopped italian parsley

Prepare the farro: wash and soak in cold water (3 parts water to 1 part farro) at least 6 hours. Drain just before using.

In a soup pot, heat the olive oil over medium heat. Add celery, fennel, and onions, and cook, stirring, until onions are translucent, about 7 minutes. Add salt and pepper. Stir in carrots, tomatoes and their juices, bay leaves, vegetable stock, tarragon, and farro, and simmer for 2 hours or until farro is soft. Stir in greens and parsley, and simmer for 3 minutes. Taste for salt and pepper and serve with pecorino and toasted garlic bread.

You can enjoy your farro mixed with beans, tomato, prosciutto, and pancetta for a thick, wintry soup...with carrots and onions...or just cook it with tomatoes.

Farro was a staple of Mediterranean diets for thousands of years, and eventually became the standard ration of the Roman Legions. Ground into a paste and cooked, it was known as "puls," an early form of polenta eaten by the Roman peasants. The Romans ate so much farro that the Greeks made fun of them as "puls-eaters." With the discovery of higher-yielding grains, the cultivation of farro diminished to just a few hundred acres in the region around Tuscany. Farro is enjoying a new global popularity today...but the Florentines have always eaten it.

LA PASTA DI

PASTIFICIO ARTIGIANO IN STRADA IN CHIANTI DAL 1893

GIOVANNI FABBRI

Pasta essiccata
a temperatura inferiore a 35°C

Oltre 100 anni fa, in un piccolo borgo nel cuore del Chianti, Giovanni Fabbri iniziò a produrre pasta, con pochi mezzi e tanta passione. Generazioni nel Pastificio Fabbri hanno intatta quella passione

...il prodotto ben fatto di dalla qualità ricavata ...ri ricca di glutine ...mente limitata

pasta, polenta
& risotti

gnocchi of polenta
with wild boar ragu

serves 6

8 cups water

pinch of salt

2 cups medium-grain cornmeal, or
   packaged polenta to make 5 cups
   cooked polenta

4 cups wild boar ragu (p. 109)

1 cup grated parmigiano

freshly ground black pepper

In a pot, bring salted water to a boil. Turn heat to low, slowly whisk in cornmeal, and cook about 45 minutes, stirring often so cornmeal does not stick to bottom of pan. It will be soft and creamy—and now you can call it polenta. (Depending on the kind of cornmeal you use, the cooking time and quantity of water required may vary.)

Gnocchi are, in this case, just spoonfuls of creamy polenta placed in a serving bowl and dressed with wild boar ragu, parmigiano, and freshly ground black pepper.

For individual servings, scoop $^1/_4$ cup ragu in the bottom of your soup bowls, top with 2 or 3 spoonfuls of polenta and a sprinkle of parmigiano; repeat. Add a salad and a cookie, and dinner is ready!

To make leftover polenta: pour while hot into a loaf pan, level, and cover. Refrigerate until firm, then slice in $^3/_4$-inch-thick pieces. Grill on a hot flat-top grill with a drizzle of olive oil, salt and pepper. Let it get crispy before flipping once. Serve as an accompaniment to vegetables, meats, or stews. You can also use leftover polenta in a casserole.

To make Tuscan chips, cut cold polenta into 2-inch squares, $^1/_4$-inch thick, and deep-fry in vegetable oil until crispy.

wild boar ragu

makes 1 gallon

3 pounds ground boar

1 pound ground lean pork

3 1/4 cups red wine, divided

1/2 cup extra virgin olive oil

2 medium yellow onions, minced

1 large carrot, minced

2 stalks celery, minced

3 cloves garlic, minced

1 cup chopped italian parsley

1 cup diced pancetta (about 1/2 pound)

salt and pepper to taste

3 bay leaves

4 or 5 juniper berries

2 tablespoons tomato paste

18 cups canned tomato purée

pinch of hot red pepper flakes

In a bowl, marinate boar and pork in 1 3/4 cups wine and refrigerate at least 3 hours.

In a large soup pot, heat olive oil. Add minced onions, carrot, celery, garlic, and parsley, and sauté over medium-high heat until onions are soft and translucent, about 10 minutes. Add marinated boar and pork, pancetta, salt and pepper. Cook, uncovered, stirring with a wooden spoon, until meat is brown, about 30 minutes. Add remaining 1 1/2 cups wine and stir, scraping the bottom of the pan. Add bay leaves, juniper berries, and tomato paste, and cook 2 more minutes. Stir in tomato purée and red pepper flakes, and simmer, covered, for 2 hours. Salt and pepper to taste.

Serve on polenta, fresh pappardelle, tagliatelle, spinach-cheese ravioli, lasagna...and, of course, toasted breads.

Meat ragu takes a few hours to cook. Talk about slow food! It freezes very well, so freeze in small portions for use later. For Ragu alla Bolognese (beef ragu), substitute beef for the boar.

risotto with
asparagus tips

serves 6 to 8

2 pounds green asparagus,
   tough ends removed

8 cups water

pinch of salt

6 tablespoons butter, divided

1 tablespoon extra virgin olive oil

1 medium yellow onion, diced

2 cups arborio rice

1 tablespoon chopped italian parsley

salt and pepper to taste

$^3/_4$ cup grated parmigiano

Wash asparagus and discard tough ends. Break off asparagus tips to about $1^1/_2$ inches long and separate from stalks.

Bring water to a boil with a pinch of salt and cook asparagus stalks until tender, about 5 minutes. Remove stalks and purée. Save cooking water on a low simmer.

Sauté asparagus tips in 2 tablespoons butter on high heat for 3 minutes and set aside.

In a wide pot, heat olive oil and 2 tablespoons butter. Add onion and cook over medium-high heat until translucent. Stir in asparagus purée and rice, and cook, adding asparagus cooking water a little at a time, until rice is al dente.

Add asparagus tips, remaining 2 tablespoons butter, parsley, salt and pepper, and serve with parmigiano.

polenta casserole with gorgonzola & mushrooms

serves 6

4 tablespoons extra virgin olive oil

4 tablespoons butter

3 small yellow onions, cut in thin crescents

6 cups sliced button mushrooms

1 tablespoon minced garlic (optional)

$^3/_4$ pound gorgonzola

3 cups half-and-half

$^3/_4$ tablespoon fresh thyme leaves

1 tablespoon chopped italian parsley

a few fresh sage leaves

salt and pepper to taste

$^1/_2$-inch-thick slices leftover polenta

1 cup grated parmigiano

Preheat oven to 350° F.

In a skillet, heat olive oil, butter, and onions and cook until onions are soft and golden. Add mushrooms and cook, stirring a few times, for 10 more minutes. Add garlic and cook 3 minutes. Stir in gorgonzola and half-and-half, and simmer until the gorgonzola melts. Add thyme, parsley, and sage, and taste for salt and pepper. Remove sauce from stove.

In a baking dish, layer sauce, then polenta. Add another layer of sauce, $^1/_2$ cup parmigiano, and polenta. Finish with a layer of sauce and the remaining parmigiano, and bake until polenta bubbles and top is crispy, about 45 minutes. Serve hot.

Polenta is to Italians what potatoes are to Idahoans. Use it for gnocchi, grilling, or casseroles. Or add sugar and milk and you have the Italian breakfast cereal!

Once upon a time in Italy, polenta was cooked in a copper pot hanging from a long chain over an open fire. It was stirred and stirred for hours with a soft wooden stick. Today, polenta has caught up with modern kitchens, and you can buy it already partially cooked. Amazing!

seafood risotto

serves 6 to 8

1 pound shrimp, peeled, and
   deveined, tails on

1 pound large bay scallops

1/2 pound calamari tubes, cut in rings,
   or calamari steak cut in 1/4-inch strips

1/2 pound fresh clams, washed in salted
   water (discard any broken or open)

1/2 pound fresh mussels, washed in salted
   water (discard any broken or open)

1 tablespoon minced garlic

3 tablespoons chopped italian parsley

1 tablespoon fresh tarragon leaves

1/4 teaspoon hot red pepper flakes

salt and pepper to taste

1/2 cup extra virgin olive oil, divided

8 cups fish or lobster stock

1/2 teaspoon saffron

1 tablespoon fresh oregano leaves

1/2 pound shallots, sliced in half-rounds

2 medium carrots, sliced in half-rounds

2 cups arborio rice

1 cup white wine

1/3 cup lemon juice

1 cup peas

1 cup sun-dried tomatoes in oil,
   drained and cut in half

1/3 cup fresh basil leaves, cut in strips

1 cup grated parmigiano

Have your seafood ready.

In a bowl, combine garlic, parsley, tarragon, red pepper flakes, salt and pepper, and 1/4 cup olive oil. Divide marinade in two bowls, placing clams and mussels in one bowl, and shrimp, scallops, and calamari in the other.

In a saucepan, bring fish stock to a low simmer with saffron and oregano.

In a wide pan, heat 1/4 cup olive oil and sauté shallots and carrots until they begin to caramelize, about 5 minutes. Add rice and cook, stirring with a wooden spoon, for 2 minutes. Add white wine and continue stirring one more minute. Gradually add warm fish stock 2 cups at a time, adding more broth as liquid absorbs.

While risotto is cooking, in a large skillet on very high heat, cook herbed shrimp, calamari, and scallops with their marinade for 5 minutes. Stir in clams and mussels with their marinade, add lemon juice, and cook for one minute. Cover and cook until clam and mussel shells open. Remove from heat, and discard any mussels or clams that do not open.

At this point, risotto should be al dente. Stir in peas, sun-dried tomatoes, basil, and cooked seafood and their juices. Add remaining stock if needed. Adjust for salt and pepper and serve immediately with parmigiano.

Life is too short to panic about risotto…so have a martini and enjoy orchestrating this seafood symphony!

spaghetti
with spicy eggplant

serves 6

2 medium eggplants, skins on,
  cut in 1-inch cubes

1 tablespoon kosher salt

1 1/4 cups extra virgin olive oil,
  divided

4 cups diced fresh tomatoes

10 canned piquillo peppers or
  3 roasted bell peppers, skins and
  seeds removed, cut in 1/2-inch strips

2 tablespoons minced garlic

2 cups salsa rossa (p. 35) or canned
  tomato sauce

1 cup fresh basil leaves, cut in strips

pinch of hot red pepper flakes

2 tablespoons fresh oregano leaves

2 tablespoons chopped italian parsley

1 pound spaghetti

shaved parmigiano

Place eggplant in colander, sprinkle with salt, and let rest for one hour.

Pat eggplant dry. In a large skillet, heat 1/4 cup olive oil on high. Add in one layer of eggplant and cook until crispy on one side. Do not stir. Turn to crisp other side. Eggplant will shrink and crisp. Repeat until all the eggplant is crispy.

In a wide pot, heat 1/4 cup olive oil, add diced tomatoes and peppers, and cook on high, stirring, for about 3 minutes. Lower heat, add garlic, and cook for 2 more minutes. Add eggplant and salsa rossa, and cook, stirring gently a couple of times. Add basil, red pepper flakes, oregano, and parsley.

In a large pot, bring salted water to boil and cook spaghetti until al dente. Drain, reserving 2 cups cooking water. Add pasta to sauce and cook over high heat 2 to 3 minutes, adding a little pasta water if needed to keep everything juicy. Serve with shaved parmigiano.

As someone once said, "No man is lonely while eating spaghetti—it requires too much attention!"

orecchiette
& broccoli rabe

serves 6 to 8

2 pounds broccoli rabe or broccolini

$^1/_2$ cup extra virgin olive oil,
   plus 2 tablespoons

6 cloves garlic, thinly sliced

2 to 4 whole dried chile peppers,
   crushed

$^1/_2$ cup breadcrumbs

1 pound orecchiette

salt and pepper to taste

$^3/_4$ cup grated pecorino toscano or
   cubed toscano fresco

Bring a large pot of salted water to a boil.

Wash broccoli rabe and break off tough ends. Cut stems in 2 or 3 slices and cook in boiling water until soft, about 5 to 6 minutes. Remove with slotted spoon, keeping the water at a boil.

In a large skillet, heat $^1/_2$ cup olive oil. Add cooked rabe and sauté until lightly browned. Add garlic, crushed chiles, and breadcrumbs and cook a few more minutes until lightly colored.

Cook orecchiette in reserved rabe water until al dente. Drain, reserving 2 cups water. Drag pasta in sauce, and cook over high heat 2 to 3 minutes, adding a little pasta water if needed. Adjust for salt and pepper.

Drizzle with 2 tablespoons olive oil, stir in pecorino, and serve.

We call it pasta strascicata or "dragged pasta" when we mix pasta with the sauce in the pot. When you drag it on high heat, the sauce sticks to the pasta much better, and the aromas come steaming out. That is pasta con amore!

ziti & vodka sauce

serves 6 to 8

6 slices pancetta, $1/8$ inch thick

1 small yellow onion, quartered

6 cups canned or fresh plum
   tomatoes, puréed

pinch of hot red pepper flakes

$1/2$ cup unflavored vodka

1 cup heavy cream

salt and pepper to taste

1 pound ziti

$3/4$ cup grated parmigiano

In a food processor, finely mince pancetta and onion together. Transfer to a heavy sauté pan and cook over medium heat until golden brown, about 15 to 20 minutes.

Add puréed tomatoes and red pepper flakes and simmer on low, partially covered, for 30 minutes. Add vodka and cook 10 more minutes. Slowly add heavy cream and bring back to simmer.

In a large pot, bring salted water to a boil and cook ziti until al dente. Drain, reserving one cup cooking water. Drag ziti in sauce, and cook over high heat 2 to 3 minutes, adding a little water if needed for moisture. Adjust for salt and pepper, and serve with parmigiano.

Pasta is "It!" The people's food. Economical, healthy, versatile, and simple.

tagliatelle with fava beans & pancetta

serves 6 to 8

2 tablespoons extra virgin olive oil

2 medium yellow onions,
  cut in thin crescents

3/4 pound thinly sliced pancetta,
  chopped

2 cups fresh, shelled, young
  fava beans*

1 pound tagliatelle

2 tablespoons chopped italian parsley

salt and pepper to taste

3/4 cup grated pecorino romano

In a large skillet, heat olive oil over medium-low heat, and sauté onions and pancetta until golden, about 20 minutes. Add fava beans and cook 4 minutes. Remove from heat.

In a large pot of boiling, salted water, cook pasta until al dente. Drain, saving 2 cups pasta water.

Bring pancetta mixture back to simmer, add pasta and the 2 cups of pasta water. Gently stir in parsley, salt and pepper, and serve with pecorino.

*If fava beans are out of season, or you cannot find them, substitute lima beans.

Fava beans make me think of summer. From Florence to Rome, Italians eat thousands of pounds of fava beans. We even have fava bean festivals! We like the fava best when they are small and tender—raw, dipped in salt, or in salads with diced pecorino, olive oil, lemon juice, and pepper. Yummy!

penne piccanti

serves 6 to 8

7 $\frac{1}{2}$ cups very ripe tomatoes

6 tablespoons extra virgin olive oil

6 cloves garlic, thinly sliced

2 to 4 whole dried chile peppers

5 sprigs italian parsley

10 leaves fresh basil

salt and pepper to taste

1 pound penne

1 teaspoon anchovy drizzle (optional)

whole parsley leaves, for garnish

In a large bowl, crush tomatoes, and set aside.

In a large skillet, heat olive oil and sauté garlic until golden. Add crushed tomatoes, whole chiles, parsley, basil, and salt and pepper. Bring to a boil and simmer until tomatoes are very soft, about 30 minutes.

In a large pot of salted water, cook pasta until al dente. Drain, drag in the sauce, and cook over high heat 2 to 3 minutes. Taste for salt and pepper, and serve with a teaspoon of anchovy drizzle. If you don't like anchovies, omit from the drizzle. Garnish with whole parsley leaves.

This recipe is a fabulous way to use over-ripe tomatoes. Make it as spicy as you like by adjusting chiles. The sauce is also very good on oiled, toasted bread. Garnish with a fresh basil leaf and a shave of parmigiano and you have a great snack or TV dinner!

anchovy drizzle

6 anchovy fillets, canned in oil

1 tablespoon capers, minced

1 tablespoon caper juice

1 whole dried chile pepper, finely crushed

4 tablespoons extra virgin olive oil

With a fork, crush the anchovy fillets, and then stir in capers and caper juice, crushed chile, and olive oil.

risotto
della nonna landi

serves 6 to 8

10 cups vegetable stock (p. 91)

6 tablespoons butter

1 large yellow onion, cut in
  thin crescents

1 pound green cabbage, thinly sliced

2 cups arborio rice

salt and white pepper

6 egg yolks

2 cups grated parmigiano

Bring stock to boil and keep at a low simmer.

In a large skillet, sauté onion in butter until translucent, about 8 minutes. Add cabbage and 5 cups stock, and cook, covered, on low heat until cabbage is very soft, about 30 minutes. If needed, add a little more stock.

Stir in rice, salt and pepper, and cook 5 minutes. Add the stock a little at a time, stirring, and cook until rice is al dente.

Transfer rice to a serving bowl. Slowly stir in egg yolks and parmigiano. Taste for salt and pepper, and serve.

Grandmother Landi was a great lady who lived on a beautiful estate in Strada in Chianti, where the town square has her name. She used to tell us stories about people, life, and food while we sat with her under her big magnolia tree overlooking the beautiful vineyards of Chianti. The tree is still there, and her granddaughter MariaLuisa sits there now. When I am home we sit there together and we remember...

fish & meat

pollo alla diavola

serves 6 to 8

3 whole chickens

$^3/_4$ cup extra virgin olive oil

3 lemons, halved, with their juices

3 tablespoons coarsely cracked
   black pepper

kosher salt

pinch of hot red pepper flakes

10 fresh sage leaves

Cut chickens open on the breast side, and arrange on a baking sheet. Flatten chickens with your hands, then rub with a drizzle of olive oil, lemon juice, pepper, salt, and red pepper flakes. Flip chickens and repeat. Arrange sage leaves and lemon halves on chickens, cover with plastic wrap, and weight with bricks, stones, or pots. Marinate at least one hour.

Secure chickens and lemons in a barbeque cage, reserving the juices. On a hot grill (a few flames are good), cook over hot coals, turning 3 or 4 times, brushing with reserved juices. Chicken should be done in 30 to 35 minutes.

Remove from grill, cut in half, and serve with oven-roasted potatoes.

oven-roasted potatoes

serves 6 to 8

5 russet potatoes, skins on

2 sprigs rosemary, cut in 2 or 3 pieces

2 fresh sage leaves

8 cloves garlic

salt and pepper to taste

$^1/_4$ cup plus 2 tablespoons extra
   virgin olive oil

$^1/_2$ cup water, if needed

Preheat oven to 350° F.

Cut potatoes in 4 or 5 pieces. In an oiled baking dish, arrange potatoes, rosemary, sage, garlic, and salt and pepper. Drizzle with $^1/_4$ cup olive oil and bake on the lower rack of the oven, turning occasionally. Add a little water after 45 minutes to keep potatoes moist. Cook until soft on the inside and crispy and golden on the outside, about 1 $^1/_4$ hours. Drizzle with 2 tablespoons olive oil and serve.

This chicken became popular at fairs in Tuscany, especially the fair at Impruneta, a small town in Chianti, for the festival of St. Luca, patron of the town. Big fires were built right on the square with oak wood, which was abundant. It is said that the dish was named after the devil because of the cooking method—over huge flames, which remind us of hell—and also because it is so peppery that those who eat it often want to send the cook to hell!

boar loin
with fennel & apples

serves 8

8 boar loins, 6 to 7 ounces each

$^1/_4$ cup plus 2 tablespoons extra
  virgin olive oil

3 sprigs rosemary, stems removed

5 fresh sage leaves, chopped

3 cloves garlic, thinly sliced

salt and pepper to taste

$^1/_2$ cup white wine, for deglazing

Prepare mustard cream sauce and set aside.

In a shallow pan, marinate loins in $^1/_4$ cup olive oil, rosemary, sage, garlic, salt and pepper while you prepare sautéed fennel and apples.

In a large skillet, heat remaining 2 tablespoons olive oil over high heat. Pan-sear the loins, browning entire surface, about 4 minutes for rare. Remove meat from pan and let rest.

Deglaze pan with $^1/_2$ cup white wine, simmering a few minutes. Add pan juices to mustard cream sauce.

Slice loin into medallions, drizzle with hot mustard cream sauce, and serve with sautéed fennel and apples.

mustard cream sauce

3 tablespoons extra virgin olive oil

3 shallots, thinly sliced

$^1/_4$ cup white wine

2 tablespoons whole-grain mustard

1 cup heavy cream

salt and pepper to taste

boar loin pan juices

In a saucepan, heat shallots in olive oil over medium heat until golden. Add wine and cook 2 more minutes. Lower heat and add mustard, cream, and salt and pepper. Add boar loin pan juices just before serving.

sautéed
fennel & apples

5 tablespoons extra virgin olive oil

4 crispy apples

2 bulbs fresh fennel, outer
  leaves removed

2 cloves garlic, thinly sliced

2 tablespoons chopped italian parsley

2 tablespoons fresh thyme leaves

salt and pepper to taste

Cut each apple into 12 slices. Slice each fennel bulb lengthwise into 8 pieces.

In a wide skillet, heat olive oil and cook fennel over medium heat until golden, about 6 to 8 minutes. Add apples and cook until golden, about 3 more minutes. Lower heat and add garlic, parsley, thyme, and salt and pepper. Cook until fennel is soft, about one more minute.

peposo
delle fornacine

serves **8**

5 pounds stew meat, cubed

12 cups canned italian chunky
   tomatoes, with their juices

8 cloves garlic

5 tablespoons peppercorns

6 tablespoons extra virgin olive oil

1 bottle chianti

salt to taste

In a container, place meat, tomatoes, garlic, and peppercorns. Cover and refrigerate at least 4 hours.

In a large stew pot, heat olive oil; add marinated meat and all the juices, and bring to a boil. Cover and simmer 2 hours. Add wine, and salt to taste. Return to a boil and cook, covered, on a low simmer for $2^{1}/_{2}$ more hours. Taste, and if meat is not melting in your mouth, cook longer. Add a little hot water if the stew is too thick.

Serve with toasted breads drizzled with olive oil and sautéed chard. And a glass of red wine, naturally. Peposo is also good on polenta and mashed potatoes.

The story: humble, of course. This dish was prepared by the fornacini *(brickmakers) of Impruneta, famous for centuries as a place where "bakers" turn dirt into amazing terra-cotta art forms. As the story goes, the brickmakers had to tend the ovens all night. They took inexpensive meat, tomatoes, garlic, and water and put everything into a pot and then into the wood ovens, just inside the door where the heat was moderate. The pot cooked all night and the next day their lunch was ready. The flavor of the wood fire gave the dish a very earthy taste. If you have a pizza oven, use it! You will feel like you are right in the heart of Tuscany. Deliciouuuus!*

bistecca alla fiorentina

serves 6

6 t-bone or porterhouse steaks,
  cut 1 1/2 to 2 inches thick
salt and freshly cracked black pepper
lemon wedges

Have grill on, with hot burning coals—
no flame.

Lay steaks on hot grill and do not touch
for 5 minutes. With a spatula, turn steaks,
and salt the cooked side. Cook 5 more
minutes, flip again and salt other side.
Done! The steak will have a crispy surface
and be rare inside.

Transfer to a serving tray; add freshly
cracked black pepper and a few drops of
lemon juice. Serve with roasted potatoes
or a simple green salad.

We Florentines are very picky about our steak. We like it simple: No oil, no marinades, no infusions, no butter—just the great flavor of the meat. A well-done steak does not exist in Tuscany, so if you like your steak well-done, your only option is to make a different choice for dinner!

The word bistecca *comes from the English "beefsteak." As the story goes, in the late 1500s there was a big party in St. Lorenzo Square in Florence to celebrate the saint, and everyone was welcome to join in the festivities. A huge spit was set up with a whole beef roasting on it. The red wine was flowing. The common people, the bourgeoisie, and, of course, the tourists—English in this case—were celebrating and having a good time. The English tasted that meat and kept asking for more and more "beefsteak! beefsteak!" Overnight, the "beefsteak" became* bistecca, *and since it was cooked in Florence,* bistecca alla fiorentina— *one of the symbols of the Florentine kitchen.*

medieval roast & artichokes

serves 8

2 1/2 pounds beef top sirloin cab

1/2 cup water, plus a little more

Preheat oven to 550° F.

Place meat in a shallow baking dish and cook on lower rack of oven for 20 minutes without turning. Remove from oven and add water to deglaze pan.

Slice meat very thinly—it will be roasted outside and rare inside. Arrange on a platter and drizzle with deglazing liquid. Serve with rosemary-sage salsa verde and fresh baby artichokes al tegame.

rosemary-sage salsa verde

2 sprigs rosemary, stems removed

6 fresh sage leaves

1/2 cup extra virgin olive oil

salt and pepper to taste

On a cutting board, finely mince rosemary and sage. Add olive oil, salt and pepper, and mix well.

fresh baby artichokes al tegame

3 lemons, halved

2 1/2 pounds fresh baby artichokes

1/2 cup extra virgin olive oil

4 bay leaves

3 sprigs rosemary

1 whole dried chile pepper (optional)

6 cloves garlic

salt and pepper to taste

3/4 cup chopped italian parsley

In a bowl of cold water, squeeze lemon juice and add the rinds.

Clean artichokes by removing a few outer leaves. Shave green from white part of the artichoke leaves upwards, in order to maintain the shape of the artichokes. With a knife, peel outer skin from stems. Immediately immerse artichokes in lemon water, weighing them down with a dish or lid to keep them submerged and prevent discoloration.

In a wide saucepan, heat the olive oil and add artichokes, lemons from water, bay leaves, rosemary, and dried chile. Sauté over moderate heat until lightly browned, adding a little water if needed. Add garlic, salt and pepper. Cover and cook, stirring occasionally, until artichokes are soft and juicy, about 30 minutes. Stir in parsley, adjust for salt and pepper, and serve.

Baby artichokes are very good raw. We dip the leaves and hearts in olive oil, vinegar, salt and pepper. Just remember to bite into only the tender white part!

affettata con arugula

fresh arugula, butter lettuce, or escarole

leftover steak or medio evo, sliced

thinly sliced parmigiano or
   pecorino toscano

extra virgin olive oil

salt and freshly cracked black pepper

a few drops of lemon juice (optional)

Should you not be able to finish your steak, save it for later and transform it into this dish.

On a serving plate, arrange greens, steak, cheese, a drizzle of olive oil, salt and pepper, and—if you like—lemon. A slice of good bread and…what else do we need?

Dinner, lunch, picnic…

Rucola, ruchetta, *rocket greens, or arugula —for Tuscans, there is nothing "gourmet" about this aromatic and peppery green! If you live in the country, you have it in your garden; if you live in the city, you take weekend car rides to the countryside, looking for field greens.*

veal chop with porcini & lemon

serves 6

6 veal chops with bone, cut 1 1/2 inches thick

3 cups milk

1/2 cup extra virgin olive oil

2 tablespoons chopped fresh oregano leaves

2 tablespoons minced garlic

1 teaspoon spanish paprika

salt and pepper to taste

Cover veal chops with milk and refrigerate at least 4 hours or overnight.

Mix together olive oil, oregano, garlic, paprika, salt and pepper, and set aside.

Drain veal chops and pat dry. Rub with herb and olive oil mixture and set aside while making porcini-lemon sauce.

Heat grill or heavy skillet to very hot and grill chops 3 to 4 minutes on each side, for rare. Spoon porcini-lemon sauce over each chop and serve with sautéed spinach. You can cook longer for well-done...but that would be sacrilege!

In Florence, we soak veal and pork in milk because we think it tenderizes the meat and turns it a beautiful pink color.

porcini-lemon sauce

2 ounces dried porcini mushrooms

1/2 cup marsala or white wine

1 cup warm water

1/2 cup butter, divided

1/4 cup chopped shallots

1/2 cup lemon juice

1 teaspoon minced garlic

1 tablespoon fresh thyme leaves

2 cups beef or veal stock

zest of 1 lemon

2 tablespoons chopped italian parsley

Soak mushrooms for one hour in marsala and warm water.

In a skillet, heat one tablespoon butter, and cook shallots until translucent. Drain porcini, reserving soaking water. Add to skillet with shallots and cook 2 to 3 minutes over medium-high heat. Stir in lemon juice, garlic, and thyme. Add stock and porcini soaking water. (Do not stir soaking water. Porcini have dirt that will have settled to the bottom.) Cook 5 minutes until sauce reduces a bit, then add lemon zest and parsley. Whisk in the rest of the butter. Sauce should look glossy.

pheasant pie

serves 6

2 pheasants, 2 1/2 pounds each, cleaned

2 medium yellow onions, cut in chunks

6 bay leaves

12 fresh sage leaves

6 tablespoons duck fat or 10 slices thinly sliced pancetta

salt and pepper to taste

8 juniper berries

3 celery stalks, coarsely chopped

2 tablespoons extra virgin olive oil

1 cup chicken stock

2 small parsnips, peeled and cut in thin strips

1 cup pearl onions

3 pears, unpeeled, thinly sliced

1 cup fresh or frozen cranberries

1 tablespoon chopped italian parsley

Preheat oven to 350° F.

Into each pheasant cavity place 3 onion chunks, one bay leaf, 2 sage leaves, one tablespoon duck fat, and salt and pepper. Rub outside with 2 tablespoons duck fat and sprinkle with salt and pepper. If you are using pancetta, place 2 slices in each cavity and lay the rest on top.

Place pheasants in a roasting pan, add remaining onion chunks, bay leaves, sage leaves, juniper berries, celery, olive oil, and chicken stock, and bake 25 minutes, basting a few times. Remove from oven while pheasant is still pink—do not over-cook! Pick meat from bones, discard bones and vegetables, and reserve juice.

In a separate pan, brown pearl onions and set aside.

Prepare biscuit topping and sauce (p. 147).

Into a 10-inch baking dish, pour one cup sauce. Distribute pheasant, parsnips, pearl onions, pears, cranberries, and parsley. Pour remaining sauce on top. With lightly floured hands, place scoops of biscuit dough about 1/2 inch thick to loosely cover mixture. Brush with melted butter or cream and bake 45 minutes or until top is golden and pie is bubbling.

biscuit topping

1 1/4 cups all-purpose flour, plus
  1/4 cup for handling

1/4 teaspoon salt

2 teaspoons baking powder

1/4 teaspoon sugar

1 cup heavy cream

In a mixing bowl, sift together dry ingredients. Fold in cream to make a soft and sticky dough. Dust with a little flour, cover, and chill until needed.

sauce

2 cups beef stock or
  pheasant roasting juice

1 cup dry vermouth

2 1/2 cups sour cream

1/2 cup heavy cream

1/4 cup honey mustard

pinch of nutmeg

salt and freshly cracked black pepper

1/4 cup chopped italian parsley

In a saucepan, simmer and reduce your stock to one cup. Add vermouth and simmer 2 minutes. Add sour cream, heavy cream, honey mustard, nutmeg, and salt and pepper to taste. Simmer on low, stirring, for 2 more minutes.

cod in zimino

serves 6

2 1/2 pounds fresh cod, deboned
    and cut in 6 pieces

1/2 tablespoon paprika

1/2 cup extra virgin olive oil,
    plus 3 tablespoons

1 medium carrot, diced

1 tender stalk celery, diced

2 leeks, white part, cut in thin rounds

4 cloves garlic, thinly sliced

salt and pepper to taste

pinch of hot red pepper flakes

1 1/2 pounds chard, blanched and
    coarsely chopped

3 cups diced ripe plum tomatoes

1/4 cup chopped italian parsley

Dust cod with paprika. Heat 1/2 cup olive oil in a wide skillet and pan-sear the cod over medium-high heat on both sides. Set aside.

In a wide saucepan, heat 3 tablespoons olive oil and sauté carrot, celery, and leeks until vegetables are lightly colored. Add garlic, salt and pepper, and red pepper flakes and cook 2 more minutes. Add chard and tomatoes and cook on low heat, stirring, about 6 minutes.

Add pan-seared cod and parsley to vegetable mixture. Cover and cook until cod is done, about 7 minutes.

Fresh cod is a luxury for Italians. Most of our cod dishes—and we eat a lot of cod—use salted cod, which is inexpensive and sold everywhere.

It appears that zimino is a contraction of the Arabic word samin and the northern Italian word cimino for cumin. Both words indicate fish soups, always with chard or spinach. You can substitute fresh spinach for the chard...and add garbanzo beans if you like.

trout on a plate

serves 6

6 (8-ounce) ruby red or rainbow
  trout fillets, skin on

salt and pepper to taste

$^3/_4$ cup extra virgin olive oil or
  clarified butter

1 cup white wine

juice and zest of 1 lemon

$^1/_2$ cup chopped italian parsley

Salt and pepper the fillets.

In a wide skillet, heat olive oil over high heat, add fillets, and sear about 1 $^1/_2$ minutes. Using a spatula, flip fish and sear the other side. (If your pan is not large enough to accommodate all the fillets, divide fish and ingredients into batches.)

Add wine, lemon juice and zest, and parsley; taste for salt and pepper. Cook 2 to 3 minutes and serve.

You can cook large shrimp the same way and serve on pasta, salad, or on top of the trout. *Ottimo*—just great!

halibut &
hazelnut sauce

serves 6

2 1/2 pounds halibut, cut in 6 chunks,
   2 1/2 inches thick

salt and pepper to taste

2 egg whites plus 2 tablespoons water,
   lightly whisked together

1/4 cup rice flour

1 1/2 cups hazelnuts, toasted, skinned,
   and finely ground

1/4 cup clarified butter or olive oil

1/4 cup chopped toasted hazelnuts,
   for garnish

Preheat oven to 350° F.

Season fish with salt and pepper. Dredge
in egg wash, then rice flour, then again in
egg wash.

Press top and bottom of fish into ground
hazelnuts.

In a wide skillet, heat butter over medium
heat and pan-sear fish 2 1/2 minutes on
each side. Place skillet in oven and cook
until fish flakes, about 7 minutes. Serve
with a drizzle of hazelnut sauce and
toasted hazelnuts.

hazelnut sauce

1/4 cup butter

1/2 cup thinly sliced shallots

1/2 cup hazelnut liqueur (frangelico)

2 tablespoons chopped italian parsley

1 tablespoon brown sugar

In a small saucepan over medium heat,
sauté shallots in butter until lightly colored. Turn up heat, add liqueur, and flambé
until flame goes out. (If you are cooking
over electric, you must ignite liqueur with
a match.) Turn to low heat and whisk in
parsley and brown sugar.

crispy lamb chops

serves 8

2 cups breading
3 eggs
salt and pepper to taste
24 small lamb chops
1/4 cup all-purpose flour
4 cups vegetable oil
2 lemons, quartered

Prepare breading and set aside.

In a shallow dish, combine eggs with salt and pepper.

Dust chops with flour, dip in egg mixture, then pat in breading.

In a skillet, heat oil to 200 to 220° F., measuring temperature with a candy thermometer. Place 4 to 5 chops at a time in the hot oil and cook about 2 minutes on each side for medium-rare. Chops should be pink on the inside, crispy on the outside. Drain on a paper towel and repeat until all chops are done.

Serve hot with a squeeze of fresh lemon juice. Especially good accompanied by verdure verdi such as black kale, spinach, or chard.

breading

1 1/2 cups breadcrumbs
1/2 cup grated parmigiano
5 sage leaves, chopped

Mix all ingredients together.

verdure verdi

2 pounds any greens
1 tablespoon extra virgin olive oil
1 clove garlic, thinly sliced
a few drops of lemon juice (optional)

Blanch greens in a little boiling, salted water. Drain, squeeze out water, and sauté with olive oil and garlic for one minute. Add a little lemon juice before serving.

If you are not going to use your greens immediately, do like the Tuscans do—squeeze into balls and refrigerate until later.

Cavolo nero, cavolo verza, bietole, cime di rapa, escarola, spinaci (*kale, green cabbage, chard, broccoli rabe, escarole, spinach*)—*we Italians eat lots of* verdure verdi. *As* contorni (*side dishes*), antipasti, *on breads, with eggs, in soups, stews, pastas, sautéed with sausages or* pancetta…

desserts

CRISTINA'S
of Sun Valley

Marmellata di Mele Cotogne

208-726-4499

520 2nd St. East Ketchum, Idaho 83340

quince jam

makes six 8-ounce jars

13 cups water
juice and peels of 5 lemons
3 pounds ripe* quince
4 cups sugar

In a large soup pot, add water, and lemon juice and peels.

Peel quince as you would an apple, then core and cut in chunks, reserving 2 tablespoons quince seeds. As you cut the quince, immediately add chunks and a handful of quince peel to lemon water, to avoid discoloration. Bring pot to a low boil, stirring a few times, and cook until quince are very soft and water is almost all absorbed, about 1½ hours. Discard lemon peels.

In a food processor, purée two-thirds of the quince mixture, leaving one-third in pot. Return purée to pot.

Bring pot to a low heat, and stir in reserved quince seeds and sugar. Simmer 25 to 35 minutes, stirring, so sugar does not burn on the bottom of the pan. Spoon one tablespoon of jam onto a plate. Let cool and tilt plate. If jam does not move, it is done.

Transfer hot jam to clean jars, and seal and sterilize according to manufacturer's instructions.

*When quince are ripe, their delicate perfume will fill your kitchen.

To make quince candy, cook the jam until very thick, spread on a baking sheet, and cool in the refrigerator. When cooled, cut in little squares and roll in sugar. Thickened jam can also be stored in a terrine and served as a pâté with pecorino—it's so good it will bring tears to your eyes! Serve sautéed quince with pork, game, or sausages. Quince is the magic apple—inedible when raw, but delicious when cooked!

cenci della gioconda

makes 30 to 40 pieces

2 1/4 cups flour, plus 1/4 cup for
    working dough

1/2 teaspoon baking powder

pinch of salt

2 eggs

1/2 cup sugar

3 tablespoons extra virgin olive oil

2 tablespoons vin santo

zest of 1 lemon or orange (optional)

4 cups vegetable oil

powdered sugar, for dusting

In a mixing bowl, add 2 1/4 cups flour, baking powder, and salt. Make a well in the center and add eggs, sugar, olive oil, vin santo, and zest. Using your hands, work mixture to form a ball.

Transfer dough ball to a floured surface and knead for 10 minutes or until dough is soft and elastic. Refrigerate for one hour.

Heat vegetable oil to 380° F., measuring oil temperature with a candy thermometer. Roll out dough until very thin, about 1/16 inch thick. Cut with a fluted pastry wheel into eccentric shapes such as strips or diamonds; then fold, knot, and twist them. Fry a few at a time, turning once, until golden and bubbly. It just takes seconds! Drain on a paper towel.

Serve in a basket sprinkled with powdered sugar. Good hot or cold.

Cenci *have many names, but the most common are* chiacchiere di monaca *(whispers of the nuns) and* nastrini di monaca *(nuns' ribbons). So, of course, we think that the nuns in the Tuscan convents must have been the inventors of this intriguing delicacy.* Cenci *were traditionally cooked on Fat Tuesday, carnival time, when people dance and masquerade in costumes and disguises. All the Tuscan coffee shops have piles of* cenci, *which look like the wild and crazy things that come at you on Fat Tuesday.*

My mother, Gioconda, loved to make cenci *with us. We laughed and ate as we cut, inventing new shapes and knots.*

sorbetto ai frutti di bosco

makes 1 quart

1 cup simple syrup

$^1/_2$ cup blueberries or blackberries

$^1/_2$ cup strawberries or huckleberries

1 $^1/_2$ cups raspberries, divided

$^1/_4$ cup chianti

$^1/_3$ cup orange juice

Prepare simple syrup.

In a food processor, purée blueberries, strawberries, and one cup raspberries with chianti and orange juice. In a mixing bowl, combine the berry purée with the simple syrup. Place mixture in an ice cream maker and spin until sorbetto is thick. Gently fold in remaining $^1/_2$ cup raspberries. Freeze overnight. Very good with panna cotta.

simple syrup

1 cup white sugar

1 cup water

In a medium saucepan, bring sugar and water to a gentle boil and simmer for 10 minutes. Cool before using or storing in a covered container.

crostata alla marmellata

makes one 10-inch tart

1 3/4 cups all-purpose flour, plus
 1/4 cup for working dough

1/4 cup sugar, plus 2 tablespoons

pinch of salt

pinch of baking powder

1/2 cup chilled butter, cubed

1 egg, plus 1 yolk

1/4 teaspoon vanilla

1 tablespoon marsala wine (optional)

1/2 tablespoon orange or lemon zest
 (optional)

3/4 cup fruit jam of your choice

Preheat oven to 350° F.

In the bowl of a stand mixer, combine 1 3/4 cups flour, 1/4 cup sugar, salt, baking powder, and chilled butter, until mixture resembles cornmeal. Add egg, yolk, and vanilla. Add marsala wine and zest, if using, and mix just until dough comes together. Transfer dough to a lightly floured surface and set aside about one-third of the dough.

Roll out the remaining dough to form an 11-inch circle. Ease into a buttered and lightly floured 10-inch tart pan with a removable bottom, and press into the bottom and along the sides. Trim the dough 1/2-inch higher than the edge of the tart pan and fold the excess to the inside of the pan so edges are thicker than the bottom. With a fork, prick a few holes on the bottom.

Spread jam evenly on crust.

With the extra dough, roll 10 ropes 1/4 inch thick for lattice top design. Arrange the ropes diagonally across the tart, pushing ends of ropes against rim and lightly pressing at intersections.

Brush rim and ropes with egg wash and sprinkle with 2 tablespoons sugar. Refrigerate 30 minutes, and then bake for 40 minutes or until lattice is golden brown. Remove crostata from pan while still warm.

egg wash

1 egg
2 tablespoons water

Whisk together egg and water until blended and set aside.

We love to make jams in Tuscany. Crostata, or "crunchy crust," is a simple, unpretentious pastry shell filled with homemade jam…great for afternoon teas. The grandmothers still use olive oil for their crusts instead of butter. That is the way it used to be, because butter was too expensive. Try it—it's very good and light.

cantuccini

makes 36 to 40 pieces

$^1/_8$ cup milk

pinch of saffron

2 cups all-purpose flour

2 teaspoons baking powder

$^1/_2$ cup sugar, plus 2 tablespoons, for dusting

pinch of salt

2 cups whole raw almonds

2 eggs

1 tablespoon honey

1 teaspoon vanilla

$^1/_4$ cup melted butter

egg wash (p. 165)

Preheat oven to 350° F.

In a saucepan, heat milk and saffron just until warm and set aside.

In a bowl, mix together flour, baking powder, $^1/_2$ cup sugar, and salt. Add the almonds. Make a well in the center of dry ingredients and add eggs, saffron-milk mixture, honey, vanilla, and cooled melted butter. Using your hands, mix all ingredients together just enough to blend.

Divide dough into thirds. Shape each third into a log 16 inches long, $^3/_4$ inch high, and 1$^1/_2$ inches wide. Transfer logs onto a cookie sheet lined with parchment paper, about 5 inches apart. Brush each log with egg wash, dust with sugar, and refrigerate for 30 minutes.

Bake for 15 to 20 minutes or until a toothpick inserted in the center comes out clean. Remove from oven and let cool.

Lower oven temperature to 275° F.

Cut the logs into diagonal $^1/_2$-inch pieces. Place back on the cookie sheet and bake again for 5 minutes. Turn once and bake for 5 more minutes. Cool and store in a jar.

In Florence, we call these cantuccini di prato, *after the bakery Mattei in Prato that has become famous for these biscotti. Cantuccini di prato are impossible to duplicate—but this recipe is close! In the typical Tuscan tradition, they are crunchy and perfect for dipping in vin santo or coffee. There are many variations, but…why?*

chocolate chip cookies

makes 36

2 3/4 cups all-purpose flour

1 teaspoon salt

2 teaspoons baking soda

1 cup butter, softened

3/4 cup sugar

3/4 cup brown sugar

2 eggs

1 teaspoon vanilla

2 cups semisweet chocolate chips

Preheat oven to 350° F.

Sift flour, salt, and baking soda together and set aside.

In the bowl of a stand mixer with a whisk attachment, cream butter and sugars. Add eggs, one at a time, mixing after each addition. Mix in the vanilla. Add dry ingredients and mix just until incorporated. Fold in chocolate chips.

Using a 1-ounce ice cream scoop, scoop and level dough, and place on a nonstick cookie sheet, 3 inches apart. Bake 7 minutes or until slightly golden. Do not brown—my cookies are slightly underbaked so they are soft and chewy.

As a good American wife, I have learned to bake chocolate chip cookies. My husband loves them, so for his birthday I make giant-sized, overbaked, and very crispy ones...because that's the way Steve likes them!

pumpkin tiramisu

serves 10

rum syrup

1 9-ounce package chocolate wafer
 cookies or chocolate graham crackers

1 15-ounce can pumpkin purée

$^1/_2$ cup sugar

$^1/_2$ cup dark brown sugar

$^1/_2$ teaspoon cinnamon

$^1/_2$ teaspoon ground ginger

$^1/_4$ teaspoon nutmeg

1$^3/_4$ cups mascarpone

1$^3/_4$ cups heavy cream

2 tablespoons unsweetened cocoa
 powder, for dusting

Prepare rum syrup.

Line the bottom of a large serving dish with 18 to 20 cookies, overlapping them slightly. Brush the cookies with half the rum syrup.

In the bowl of a stand mixer with a whisk attachment, combine the pumpkin puree with the sugar, brown sugar, cinnamon, ginger, and nutmeg. Add the mascarpone and cream and beat on medium until peaks form. Do not overbeat. Spread half the pumpkin mixture evenly over the cookies.

Add another layer of cookies on top of the pumpkin, again overlapping them slightly. Drizzle with the rest of the syrup and cover with the remaining pumpkin mixture. Decorate with extra cookies and dust with cocoa powder. Refrigerate, covered. Serve cold.

rum syrup

$^1/_2$ cup water

$^1/_3$ cup sugar

2 tablespoons dark rum

In a small saucepan, combine the water, sugar, and rum and bring just to boil. Remove from heat.

goo cookies

makes 30

$^1/_2$ cup cake flour, plus 2 tablespoons

1 teaspoon baking powder

$^1/_4$ teaspoon salt

2 $^1/_2$ cups semisweet chocolate chips

4 tablespoons butter

1 $^3/_4$ cups brown sugar

4 eggs

1 tablespoon vanilla

8 1.4-ounce heath bars, chopped into $^1/_4$-inch strips

2 cups hazelnuts, skin on or off

Preheat oven to 350° F.

Sift together cake flour, baking powder, and salt and set aside.

Over a double boiler, melt chocolate chips and butter, stirring with a spatula and being careful not to overheat. Cool to lukewarm.

In the bowl of a stand mixer with a whisk attachment, whisk brown sugar and eggs on high speed for 5 minutes. Add vanilla and whisk 5 more minutes. Add chocolate chip mixture and whisk 5 minutes. Very important: keep the motor running on high speed for the 15 consecutive minutes it takes to do these 3 steps. No stopping!

Turn the motor off and quickly add the sifted ingredients. Mix on low speed until just incorporated, then fold in heath bars and hazelnuts.

Using a 1-ounce ice cream scoop, scoop and level dough, then place about 4 inches apart on a cookie sheet lined with parchment paper. Let cookies rest 15 minutes before baking. Bake for 8 minutes, remove from oven, and let cool completely before storing. These cookies are insanely good—but very gooey—when they are hot. Store flat, in layers, with parchment paper in between.

Goo cookies are as tricky as they are tasty. I do not remember where we found the recipe, but I do remember how long it took us to discover the trick. A customer of ours once said, "I read recipes the same way I read science fiction. I get to the end and think, 'Well, that's not going to happen!'" These fabulous cookies are going to happen—but only if you follow the instructions exactly! Call us if they don't. We will be here.

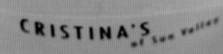

CRISTINA'S... of Sun Valley
208-726-4499

gelato di zabaione

makes 1 quart

2 cups heavy cream

2 cups zabaione

In a bowl, mix cream and zabaione together until well blended. Churn in ice cream maker until stiff, about 40 minutes.

zabaione

8 egg yolks

1 cup sugar

1/3 cup marsala

Whisk egg yolks, sugar, and marsala together over a double boiler or medium-hot water bath until sauce thickens to the consistency of pudding, about 5 to 10 minutes.

Cool zabaione over an ice bath or refrigerate overnight.

There is nothing so wrong that gelato cannot fix it!

zuppa inglese

serves 6 to 8

peel of 2 lemons

3 cups milk

7 coffee beans

$^1/_3$ cup sugar, plus 2 tablespoons

$^1/_4$ cup all-purpose flour

1 $^1/_2$ cups powdered sugar

8 egg yolks

18 ladyfingers

$^3/_4$ cup alchermes di firenze (p. 183)

Using a sharp knife, peel skin from 2 lemons, cutting around the circumference like you would an apple. Be careful not to get too much of the white.

In a saucepan, heat the milk, lemon peel, and coffee beans just to a boil; then remove from heat.

In a large bowl, whisk together sugar, flour, and powdered sugar. Whisk yolks into the dry mixture. Slowly whisk in the hot milk. Return mixture to saucepan and cook over medium heat, stirring constantly, until thickened. Remove from heat, discard lemon peel, and let cool.

Dip ladyfingers in the alchermes, and then arrange them on the bottom of a dessert bowl. Cover with half the custard, then repeat layers.

Refrigerate at least 30 minutes and serve cold.

The only English thing about this dessert is the name. It was invented by the farmers, housekeepers, and cleaning ladies of Fiesole who were hired to work in the beautiful villas rented to English tourists. They created la zuppa *to reuse assorted biscotti after tea parties—*la zuppa *(the soup), because it is an eat-with-a-spoon dessert.*

torta al gianduiotto

makes one 8-inch cake

$^3/_4$ cup unsweetened chocolate

$^1/_2$ cup butter

$^2/_3$ cup sugar, plus 2 tablespoons

3 eggs, separated

1$^1/_2$ teaspoons hazelnut liqueur
  (frangelico)

$^3/_4$ cup cake flour

$^1/_3$ cup hazelnuts, toasted, skinned,
  and finely ground

12 whole hazelnuts, toasted, for garnish

Prepare syrup and gianduia mousse in advance (p. 181).

Preheat oven to 350° F.

In a double boiler, melt chocolate, stirring, and set aside.

In the bowl of a stand mixer with a paddle attachment, cream butter and $^2/_3$ cup sugar until light and fluffy. Add egg yolks, one at a time, mixing and scraping bowl after each addition. With the stand mixer on low speed, add melted chocolate and frangelico. Mix in flour and ground hazelnuts.

In a separate bowl, whip egg whites to soft peaks while gradually adding the 2 tablespoons sugar. By hand, fold whites into cake mixture. Pour batter into a lightly buttered and floured 8-inch cake pan and bake for 25 minutes, or until a toothpick inserted in center of cake comes out with crumbs on it (we want it to be gooey and underbaked). Remove from oven and cool. Remove from pan and cut in 2 layers.

Place bottom layer on a serving dish, soak with syrup, and top with half the gianduia mousse. Add second cake layer, soak with remaining syrup, and top with rest of gianduia mousse. Garnish with whole hazelnuts, and refrigerate until ready to serve.

syrup

$^1/_3$ cup water

$^1/_4$ cup sugar

$^1/_2$ cup frangelico

Bring ingredients to boil and simmer until sugar dissolves. Set aside.

gianduia mousse

1 $^1/_2$ cups coarsely chopped
   gianduia chocolate

$^1/_2$ cup coarsely chopped
   bittersweet chocolate

4 tablespoons butter

$^1/_4$ cup hazelnut liqueur (frangelico)

2 cups heavy cream, whipped to stiff
   peaks and chilled

In a double boiler, melt gianduia, bittersweet chocolate, butter, and frangelico. Cool to room temperature, then fold into whipped cream and chill.

Gianduia mousse is good on berries and tarts, with cookies or vanilla cakes...or ice-cold with a drizzle of espresso or hot chocolate sauce. What can I say? I love gianduia!

alchermes di firenze

makes about 7 cups

4 teaspoons cinnamon

2 scant tablespoons coriander seeds

2 teaspoons cochineal or 1 5-ounce package candied pink rose petals

1 teaspoon mace

1 teaspoon whole cloves

2 teaspoons dried orange peel or 3 teaspoons freshly grated orange zest

1 teaspoon anise seed

10 pods cardamom

$1/2$ vanilla bean, cut in 3 pieces

3 cups 100-proof everclear alcohol or unflavored vodka

$3^1/2$ cups cold water

$2^3/4$ cups sugar

$1/2$ cup rosewater

With a mortar and pestle, grind together all spices except vanilla bean.

In a lidded jar, place ground spices, vanilla bean, alcohol, and $1^1/2$ cups cold water and let rest for about 2 weeks, shaking once a day.

After 2 weeks, dissolve sugar in 2 cups water and add to the infusion. Shake . . . shake . . . shake and let rest one more day. Filter with a triple layer of cheesecloth, add rosewater, and taste to see if you like it.

Use alchermes for cookie dipping, or for brushing or soaking sponge cake or ladyfingers. Also good hot on a cold winter night.

Originally used to color Florentine textiles, the red dye prepared from the dried bodies of the female cochineal insect is today used as a food coloring. It is believed that the Italian name alchermes *was derived from the Spanish* alquermes, *which came from the Arabic* quirmiz, *for scarlet.*

Alchermes di Firenze was created for the Medici by their alchemist, and they were crazy about it! They jealously guarded the recipe, which they called elisir di lunga vita, *or "elixir of long life."*

pavlovas

makes 33 to 35

2 cups egg whites, at room temperature

1/4 teaspoon salt

2 1/2 cups sugar

2 tablespoons red wine vinegar

1 tablespoon cornstarch

Preheat oven to 350° F.

In the bowl of a stand mixer with a whisk attachment, whip egg whites and salt on medium until foamy.

Continue whipping and add sugar very, very slowly. Add vinegar and cornstarch and whip mixture on high speed until stiff and glossy, about 5 minutes.

Spoon 1/2 cup mixture at a time onto a cookie sheet lined with parchment paper, keeping pavlovas about 3 inches apart. Do not spread or flatten—they should look rough and spiky.

Bake on middle rack of oven for 8 minutes, then reduce oven temperature to 300° F. and bake for 25 to 30 minutes more. Pavlovas should be golden and puffed, with a crispy top.

Turn off oven, crack the door, and let pavlovas sit inside for at least 4 hours for a crispy inside. If you prefer a chewy inside, remove from oven, cool on a rack, and serve. You can make pavlovas at least two days ahead, and store them on a rack at room temperature.

Serve with lemon mousse, fresh berries, and lemon drizzle.

lemon mousse

Mix together 1/3 cup lemon curd and 2/3 cup whipped cream.

lemon drizzle

Mix together lemon curd and lemon mousse 50/50. Add lemon juice to your taste.

lemon curd

1 cup sugar

6 egg yolks

1/2 cup lemon juice

1/2 cup butter

In a saucepan, combine sugar and egg yolks. Gradually whisk in lemon juice.

Cook on low heat, stirring constantly, until mixture is thick enough to coat the back of a spoon. It should have the consistency of mayonnaise.

Add butter and stir until dissolved.

A pavlova is mostly air. It was created in honor of the great Russian ballerina, Anna Pavlova, who enthralled audiences with her light and airy performances when she visited Australia and New Zealand in the 1920s. Chefs in both countries vied to honor her with their confections. As the story goes, one Australian hotel chef concocted a large meringue cake for afternoon tea, and someone said, "It's as light as Pavlova!" The rest is history.

breakfast

eggs benedict

serves 6

12 slices black forest ham
drop of white vinegar
12 eggs
6 english muffins

Prepare hollandaise and keep warm.

Heat the ham in a sauté pan until hot, and set aside.

Fill a large, wide pan to the rim with water, add a drop of white vinegar, and bring to a low boil. Drop 2 to 4 eggs at a time into the boiling water and cook $2^{1}/_{2}$ minutes for soft, or to your taste.

Toast the English muffins. On each muffin half, place a slice of ham and an egg. Drizzle with hollandaise and serve.

Tricky…but oh so good!

hollandaise

Serves 6

1 tablespoon water
5 egg yolks
1 cup butter, cubed
juice of 1 lemon
white pepper
salt
2 dashes tabasco
$^{1}/_{2}$ teaspoon worcestershire

In a double boiler, make sure that the water in the bottom pan touches the top pan, then place over medium heat. Put one tablespoon of water in top pan, and when it begins to steam, whisk in the egg yolks for about 30 seconds. Add the butter a little at a time, whisking constantly until mixture is thick. Still whisking, slowly add the lemon juice, white pepper, salt, tabasco, and worcestershire.

Serve over poached eggs, steamed asparagus, grilled tomatoes, wilted spinach…

german pancake

serves 4

5 eggs

1²/₃ cups milk

¹/₄ cup sugar

1¹/₂ cups all-purpose flour

2 fuji apples

1 cup orange juice

6 tablespoons butter, divided

powdered sugar, berries, and fresh
  mint leaves for garnish

maple syrup

apple seasoning

¹/₄ cup granulated sugar

1 tablespoon cinnamon

1 teaspoon nutmeg

Combine.

Preheat oven to 450° F.

In a bowl, whisk eggs, milk, and sugar. Add flour all at once and whisk just enough to combine, leaving lumps. Set aside.

Core apples and cut in ¹/₈-inch slices, leaving skin on. Cover with orange juice and set aside.

Preheat a 6-inch steel skillet in the oven for 10 minutes. Remove from oven and add 1¹/₂ tablespoons butter to evenly coat bottom of skillet. Add ¹/₄ of the apples, sprinkle with one tablespoon apple seasoning, and cover with scant one cup pancake batter. Place skillet immediately in oven on the bottom rack, or on a pizza stone, and bake until edges of cake have a dark golden color, about 12 minutes. Repeat for remaining pancakes.

Remove from oven and flip upside down onto a warm serving plate. Dust edges with powdered sugar, garnish with a few berries and a mint leaf, and serve with maple syrup.

toast, jam & caffelatte

serves 2

6 slices assorted breads
unsalted butter, on a beautiful dish
your favorite homemade jams
   or marmalades
2 caffelattes

Toast the bread, and spread with butter
and jam. Have your caffelatte hot...and
hopefully the newspaper has been deliv-
ered to your door. Enjoy your breakfast!

We Florentines drink our caffelattes in the
morning because we think it stimulates
our nerves, clears our minds, and makes
our imaginations livelier.

torta pasqualina

makes one 10-inch pie

2 cups all-purpose flour

7 ounces (14 tablespoons) chilled butter, cubed

pinch of salt

3 tablespoons ice water

2 eggs, plus 2 yolks

3 tablespoons balsamic vinegar

12 thin slices baked ham or prosciutto cotto

3 cups fresh ricotta

6 hard-boiled eggs, soft stage

egg wash (p. 165)

Preheat oven to 375° F.

In a food processor with a blade attachment, combine flour, butter, and salt until it resembles cornmeal. Add water, eggs, yolks, and balsamic vinegar, and process just until mixture comes together. Form into a ball, wrap in plastic, and refrigerate 15 minutes.

Prepare gruyère sauce and spinach filling (p. 197).

On a lightly floured surface, roll two-thirds of dough into a 17-inch round, reserving one-third. Ease dough into a buttered and lightly floured 10-inch springform pan, leaving a 1-inch overhang. Roll remaining one-third into a 10-inch round for top of pie.

Layer bottom crust with half the spinach mixture, 6 slices ham, and half the ricotta. Arrange the hard-boiled eggs end-to-end in a circle, pressing them in. Repeat spinach, ham, and ricotta layers and top with the crust top. Fold overhang back over the top, and crimp to seal.

Brush sides and top of pie with egg wash. Place springform on a baking sheet, and bake until top is golden brown, about one hour. Let rest 10 minutes before transferring to serving dish. Slice and serve with a drizzle of gruyère sauce.

This pie is traditionally served in Florence for Easter.

As we Italians say, "Natale con tuoi, Pasqua con chi vuoi." ("Christmas with family, Easter with whomever you choose.") Easter weekend is the beginning of spring, and everyone leaves their house and goes outside. Bicyclists start cruising the back roads of the Chianti, people gather for picnics and outdoor games . . . and the hunt begins for tender spring greens.

spinach filling

2 tablespoons extra virgin olive oil

1 large yellow onion, cut in
   thin crescents

3 cups (3 pounds raw) blanched
   spinach, coarsely chopped

2 tablespoons chopped italian parsley

pinch each of fresh thyme
   and marjoram

salt and pepper to taste

2 cups grated parmigiano

pinch of nutmeg

2 eggs

In a sauté pan, heat olive oil; add onion and cook until lightly colored, about 5 minutes. Add spinach, parsley, thyme, marjoram, and salt and pepper. Cook a few more minutes, then transfer to a mixing bowl, and mix in parmigiano, nutmeg, and eggs. Set aside.

gruyère sauce

$^1/_2$ cup grated gruyère

1 cup white sauce

Add gruyère to hot white sauce.

white sauce

makes about 1 cup

4 tablespoons butter

2 tablespoons all-purpose flour

1 $^1/_4$ cups milk

$^1/_4$ white onion, uncut, for flavor

1 clove

1 bay leaf

pinch of nutmeg

pinch of white pepper

1 fennel seed

Melt the butter on low heat. Whisk in the flour and blend until mixture smells like popcorn, about 2 to 3 minutes. Slowly whisk in milk. Add the onion, clove, bay leaf, nutmeg, white pepper, and fennel seed and stir over low heat until thick and smooth. Discard the onion and clove. Strain the mixture through a fine strainer. Add a little more milk if you like a looser consistency.

uova al tegamino

serves 2

2 teaspoons extra virgin olive oil

4 eggs

$^1/_4$ teaspoon truffle oil

$^1/_2$ ounce (or as much as you like) fresh
   black or white truffle

salt and freshly ground black pepper
   to taste

In a 2-egg fry pan, heat one teaspoon olive oil until hot but not smoking. Separate whites from yolks of 2 eggs and drop whites only into the pan. When the whites are almost done—about one minute—drop the yolks in the center of the whites. Cover and finish cooking, about 2 minutes. Drizzle eggs with a drop of truffle oil, garnish with 2 or 3 shaves of fresh truffle, and add salt and freshly ground black pepper. (Prepare both servings simultaneously if you want to eat together!)

Serve in the pan with bread, which you will "drown" in the yolks.

My father, Emilio, loves this dish, but we don't always have truffles. So he scoops some fresh, hot tomato sauce on his eggs and tops them with basil or parmigiano.

cristina's eggs

serves 6

6 medium vine-ripened tomatoes,
  cut in half widthwise

$1/2$ tablespoon minced garlic

3 tablespoons extra virgin olive oil,
  divided

pinch of salt and pepper

drop of white vinegar

I pound fresh baby spinach

6 slices country bread, cut in half

12 eggs

6 drops tar (optional)

Marinate tomatoes in garlic, 2 tablespoons olive oil, and salt and pepper.

In a large, wide pan, bring about 2 inches of water to a boil with the drop of white vinegar.

While tomatoes are marinating, sauté spinach over high heat with one tablespoon olive oil. Set aside and keep warm.

In the same skillet, char the tomatoes.

Toast the bread and drizzle with olive oil.

Before you poach the eggs, have your plates warm and ready: on each plate, place 2 halves toasted bread, and top with tomato and a scoop of spinach.

Drop 6 eggs at a time into the boiling water and poach $2^1/2$ minutes for soft eggs. To serve, arrange one hot, perfect poached egg on top of each stack. Drizzle with juice from tomato pan if you have any, or a drop of tar.

These are my eggs...and you will create your own eggs with your favorite toppings.

tar

4 cups balsamic vinegar

juice of $1/2$ lemon

I tablespoon honey

In a heavy-bottomed saucepan, bring balsamic vinegar to a boil and simmer until it reduces to one cup, about 15 to 20 minutes. Add lemon juice and honey, and mix well. Store at room temperature and it will last forever.

Tar is very good on salads, pastas, meats, and fish...but be very frugal when using. One or two drops and no more!

We are cheating, of course, in trying to duplicate the most expensive balsamic vinegar from Modena, which is aged for hundreds of years. But as we say, "Si fa quel che si puo"... "We do what we can!"

spinach & bacon quiche

makes one 10-inch quiche

1 cup chilled butter, cubed

$3^{1}/_{2}$ cups all-purpose flour

$^{1}/_{4}$ teaspoon salt

$^{1}/_{2}$ cup dry white wine

1 egg

$^{1}/_{4}$ cup vegetable oil

4 cups dried beans

6 eggs

2 cups heavy cream

salt and pepper to taste

Preheat oven to 350° F.

In a food processor with a blade attachment, combine butter, flour, and salt and process until mixture resembles cornmeal. Add wine, egg, and oil and process just until dough comes together.

Divide dough in half, form into 2 balls, wrap in plastic, and refrigerate one for 30 minutes (freeze the other for use later.)

On a lightly floured surface, roll out one dough ball into a round approximately 16 inches in diameter. Ease the dough into a lightly buttered and floured springform pan with fluted edge, trim edges, and prick a few holes in the bottom with a fork. Line the crust with aluminum foil, pressing it gently into the corners and edges, and cover with dried beans for weight. Bake until golden, about 30 minutes. Remove beans and foil and set crust aside while you prepare filling.

To assemble quiche, scoop filling into crust.

Whisk together eggs, cream, and salt and pepper.

Pour egg mixture over filling, dispersing evenly. Bake for about one hour and 20 minutes (check after one hour). Quiche should be puffed up, golden brown, and firm in the center. Remove from oven and let stand 10 minutes before cutting.

Fillings for quiche have no boundaries! Vary according to your taste.

Cut into little squares, quiche also makes a great appetizer.

filling

2 cups chopped yellow onion

$^{1}/_{2}$ pound sliced bacon, chopped

1 pound fresh spinach,
    coarsely chopped

1 tablespoon fresh thyme leaves

1 tablespoon chopped italian parsley

$^{1}/_{4}$ pound gruyère, cut in small cubes

In a large sauté pan over low heat, cook onions and chopped bacon until bacon is crispy and onions are lightly colored and translucent. Add spinach and thyme and cook, stirring a few more minutes. Transfer to a mixing bowl, add parsley and gruyère, and mix well.

breads

biga

makes 1 quart

starter

4 cups flour

2 cups warm water

$1/2$ cup white grape juice or white wine

feeder

3 cups flour

$1 1/2$ cups water, at room temperature

In a stand mixer with a dough hook, mix all starter ingredients just enough to incorporate, no longer than one minute. Bubbles and lumps of flour will be visible. Transfer to a container large enough to hold double the volume. Cover with plastic and let sit at room temperature at least 2 hours. Refrigerate.

Every day for 3 days feed the starter, stirring in one cup flour and $1/2$ cup water. The starter will double in size over the next 3 days, and be ready to use.

The biga will keep for a long time if kept refrigerated in an airtight container. If you do not use the biga every day, feed it every day. If you do not use within 5 days, discard half the mixture and add another 2 cups of flour and one cup water. This will keep the biga alive.

Italians say that bread is like il campanile (the bell tower). Every town has its own and claims that theirs is more beautiful and far better than the one in the neighboring town.

ciabatta

makes 2 loaves

$1/2$ teaspoon dry yeast

$1 1/2$ cups warm water

3 cups high-gluten bread flour

1 cup biga

$1/2$ tablespoon salt

In the bowl of a kitchen aid with a dough hook, dissolve yeast in the warm water. Add the flour and biga, and mix on low speed until dough begins to pull away from the sides of the bowl, about one minute. Add a little more flour only if the dough does not pull away from the sides of the bowl. Mix for 10 minutes on medium-high speed, add salt, and mix one more minute. Dough should be very soft.

Transfer dough to a well-oiled bowl. Cover with a damp cloth and let rise in a warm spot until doubled in volume, about 2 hours.

After the first rise, transfer dough to a lightly floured baking sheet. Divide dough in two without kneading, dust with flour, and let rise again (uncovered) for 45 minutes.

Preheat oven to 350° F.

Bake for 25 minutes or until the bread is golden brown and sounds hollow when tapped. Remove from oven and let cool before slicing.

Ciabatta is a chewy bread with holes. It is important that the proportions and procedure are correct—too much flour or too much kneading will change the consistency and rid your bread of its characteristic air bubbles! Ciabatta translates literally to "old, broken-down slipper," and if you look at these loaves just right, you can see the resemblance!

flatbread

makes 20 to 24 pieces

pizza skin dough balls (p. 217)
2 tablespoons butter, melted
2 roma tomatoes, sliced paper-thin
$1/4$ red onion, sliced paper-thin
15 sage leaves, cut in pieces

Preheat oven to 350° F.

With a rolling pin, on a lightly floured surface, roll pizza skin dough balls until very thin. Brush with melted butter, then cut into irregular shapes with a knife or roller. Place on a lightly floured baking sheet. On each piece arrange a few slices of tomato, onion, and sage leaves.

Bake for 3 minutes or until golden. Let cool. Flatbread will be crispy…and as delicate as feathers! Store, uncovered, in a basket at room temperature.

prune-walnut bread

makes 2 loaves

1 tablespoon dry yeast

2 cups warm water

2 cups biga (p. 207)

4 tablespoons honey

1 1/2 cups buckwheat flour

6 cups high-gluten bread flour

1 tablespoon salt

1 cup walnuts

1 cup raisins

1 1/2 cups prunes, pitted

In the bowl of a stand mixer with a dough hook, dissolve yeast in warm water. Add biga, honey, buckwheat flour, and high-gluten flour, and mix on low. While mixing, add salt. Continue mixing until dough begins to pull away from sides of the bowl, about 3 minutes. If dough is too sticky, add more flour, 1/4 cup at a time, until dough begins to ball up. Continue to mix on medium-high for 3 minutes.

Add walnuts, raisins, and prunes, and mix on low speed for 30 seconds.

Transfer dough to a well-oiled bowl. Cover with a damp cloth and let rise in a warm spot until doubled in volume, about 2 hours.

After the first rise, transfer dough to a lightly floured surface and divide in two. Form each half into an oblong loaf, and dust with flour. Place loaves on a floured baking sheet and let rise again until doubled in volume, about 2 hours. After dough has risen for a second time, make a lengthwise slash on top of the dough with a bread knife, being careful to cut no more than 1/2 inch deep.

Preheat oven to 350° F.

Bake for one hour, until bread is golden brown and sounds hollow when tapped. Remove from oven and let cool.

schiacciata con uva

makes one 12-inch schiacciata

1 loaf ciabatta dough, risen once (p. 207)
2 cups red or white grapes, as long as
    they are juicy
1/2 cup sugar
2 sprigs rosemary, stems removed
1 tablespoon extra virgin olive oil

Preheat oven to 500° F.

Place ciabatta dough on a lightly
floured surface and gently shape into a
ball. Dust with flour and let rise one
hour. Using your fingertips, very gently
push dough from center out. Stretch
the circle until 12 inches in diameter,
leaving bumps and irregularities in.

Distribute the grapes, crushing them
into the dough. Sprinkle with sugar and
rosemary, and drizzle with olive oil.
Transfer to a pizza paddle and place in
the oven on a pizza stone or floured
baking sheet.

Bake for 6 to 7 minutes or until top is
golden in spots, and sugar is caramelized
and crispy.

*Serve hot with cheese for breakfast, or
later with wine while you are talking to
your lover...or sitting on your balcony
looking at the sky...*

apricot-hazelnut bread

makes 2 loaves

1 tablespoon dry yeast

2 cups warm water

2 tablespoons molasses

2 tablespoons honey

$^1/_2$ tablespoon butter, melted

4 tablespoons rolled oats

2 cups biga (p. 207)

6 cups high-gluten bread flour

$^1/_2$ tablespoon salt

1$^1/_2$ cups dried apricots

1 cup whole hazelnuts, skins on

In the bowl of a stand mixer with a dough hook, dissolve yeast in warm water. Add molasses, honey, butter, rolled oats, biga, and flour. Mix on low, adding salt. Continue mixing until dough begins to pull away from sides of the bowl, about 3 minutes. If dough is too sticky, add more flour, $^1/_4$ cup at a time, until dough begins to ball up. Continue to mix on medium-high for 3 minutes.

Add apricots and hazelnuts and mix on low speed for 30 seconds.

Transfer dough to a well-oiled bowl, cover with a damp cloth, and let rise in a warm spot until doubled in volume, about 2 hours.

After the first rise, transfer dough to a lightly floured surface, and divide in two. Form each half into a round loaf, dust with flour, and place on a baking sheet. Let rise again until doubled in volume, about 2 hours. After dough has risen for a second time, make 5 concentric slashes with a bread knife on top of the dough, being careful to cut no more than $^1/_2$ inch deep.

Preheat oven to 350° F.

Bake for one hour, or until bread is golden brown and sounds hollow when tapped. Remove from oven and let cool.

pizza skins

makes ten 12-inch skins

$^1/_2$ tablespoon dry yeast

$2^1/_4$ cups warm water

5 cups 00 italian flour or
   all-purpose flour

1 tablespoon salt

$^1/_2$ cup flour for dusting and rolling skins

In the bowl of a stand mixer with a blade attachment, dissolve yeast in the warm water. Add flour and salt, and mix until dough clumps together, about 3 minutes. Transfer to a lightly floured surface and knead for about 5 minutes or until dough is soft and elastic. Place in a bowl, dust with flour, cover with a tea towel, and let rest in a draft-free place for at least one hour or until double in volume.

Punch down the dough to its original size, then transfer to a lightly floured surface. Divide the dough into 10 balls, dust with flour, cover with a towel and let rest for about 30 minutes. Working with one ball at a time, flatten the dough to form a circle. Using the heel of your hand and working from the center of the ball outwards, stretch it as much as you can, dusting with flour as you go. (Or use a rolling pin to reach a 12-inch skin.) If you want to save the skin for later, precook at 550° F. for 2 minutes, then cool, wrap in plastic, and freeze.

To use immediately, top with your favorite ingredients and bake at 550° F. for 5 to 6 minutes or until crispy.

For the record, Italians eat more than just pizza and lasagna! Gelato…pasta…and we even take baths in olive oil! Just kidding!

multigrain bread

makes 2 loaves

1 3/4 cups 9-grain cereal

1/2 cup rolled oats

1/2 cup sunflower seeds

1/2 cup flax seeds

2 cups cold water

1 1/2 tablespoons yeast

1 1/4 cups warm water

1/2 tablespoon molasses

3/4 cup buttermilk

4 tablespoons brown sugar

2 tablespoons honey

2 cups high-gluten bread flour

4 cups whole wheat flour

1 tablespoon salt

1/2 cup each 9-grain cereal, oats, sunflower seeds, and flax seeds, for topping

In a large bowl, soak 9-grain cereal, oats, sunflower seeds, and flax seeds in 2 cups cold water for 2 hours.

In the bowl of a stand mixer with a dough hook, dissolve yeast in the warm water. Add molasses, buttermilk, brown sugar, honey, soaked grain mixture, and both flours. Mix for 3 minutes on low speed, until dough begins to pull away from the sides of the bowl. If dough is too sticky, add more flour, 1/4 cup at a time, until the dough begins to ball up. Mix on medium-high for 2 minutes while adding salt.

Transfer dough to a well-oiled bowl. Cover with a damp cloth and let rise in a warm spot until doubled in volume, about one hour.

Combine topping ingredients.

After the first rise, transfer dough to a lightly floured surface, and divide in two. Form each half into an oblong loaf. Brush the tops with cold water, then press into topping mix, rolling gently so the grains stick to the loaf. Place the loaves on a floured baking sheet and let rise again for 40 minutes.

Preheat the oven to 350° F.

After dough has risen for a second time, make a lengthwise slash with a bread knife, being careful to cut no more than 1/2 inch deep.

Bake the dough for one hour or until the bread is golden grown and sounds hollow when tapped. Remove from the oven and let cool.

index

Metric Conversion Chart

Liquid and Dry Measures

U.S.	Canadian	Australian
1/4 teaspoon	1 mL	1 ml
1/2 teaspoon	2 mL	2 ml
1 teaspoon	5 mL	5 ml
1 Tablespoon	15 mL	20 ml
1/4 cup	50 mL	60 ml
1/3 cup	75 mL	80 ml
1/2 cup	125 mL	125 ml
2/3 cup	150 mL	170 ml
3/4 cup	175 mL	190 ml
1 cup	250 mL	250 ml
1 quart	1 liter	1 litre

Temperature Conversion Chart

Fahrenheit	Celsius
250	120
275	140
300	150
325	160
350	180
375	190
400	200
425	220
450	230
475	240
500	260